1984

Padre Pio

Padre Pio

Rev. John A. Schug, Capuchin

FRANCISCAN HERALD PRESS
1434 WEST 51st STREET • CHICAGO, 60609

Imprimi Potest:
Very Rev. Gabriel Bartoszewski, O.F.M. Cap.
Warsaw, Poland
April 14, 1975

Nihil Obstat:
Rev. Armand Dasseville, O.F.M. Cap.
Censor Deputatus

Imprimatur:
      Bernard J. Ganter, D.D.
Bishop of Tulsa
June 9, 1976

Made in the United States of America.

Reprint. Originally published: Huntington, Ind.: Our Sunday Visitor,
1976.
1. Pio, Padre, 1887 - 1968.
2. Capuchins—Italy—Biography. I. Title.
[BX4705.P49S38 1983]
271'.36'0924 [B]

ISBN 0-8199-0864-9
Library of Congress Catalog Card Number: 83-8847

Cover Design by James E. McIlrath

First Published, 1976
Revised Edition, 1979
Second Printing of 1979 Edition, May, 1980
Third Printing of 1979 Edition, May, 1983

CONTENTS

ACKNOWLEDGMENTS

A host of very dear friends have made this book possible. Through a very generous donation by Miss Dorothy Gaudiose, herself an author of a book on Padre Pio, I was able to do most of my research in San Giovanni Rotondo. Also, I am most grateful to Joseph R. Ziegler of Tulsa, Mr. and Mrs. Clyde Walker of Broken Arrow, Oklahoma, and Mrs. Francesco Martinez of Laredo, Texas, for their financial assistance which enabled me to take full advantage of my trip to Italy.

Of course I am indebted to my Capuchin Provincial and General Superiors for their permission to travel to Italy. Father Robert Dabrowski, Capuchin, my local superior, had to bear the burden of my parochial work for two full months.

In Rome, Father Bernardino of Siena, Capuchin, the Postulator General for the Cause of Padre Pio, gave me precious guidance in my work and his blessing on my completed manuscript. I am grateful for the kind permission of the Capuchins in San Giovanni Rotondo, where Padre Pio spent most of his life, to quote extensively from Volume I of the *EPISTOLARIO,* which contains the correspondence between Padre Pio and his spiritual directors. The Capuchins also gave their permission for me to quote from the *DIARIO,* the diary of Padre Agostino, Padre Pio's spiritual director, and from *THE*

VOICE OF PADRE PIO, an attractive quarterly magazine published by the Capuchins in San Giovanni Rotondo.

Similarly, I am grateful to Mr. Thomas A. Nelson, of Tan Books and Publishers, Inc., who gave me permission so graciously and encouragingly to cite ten references to *PADRE PIO — THE STIGMATIST,* by Father Carty. That runaway best seller is still an extremely popular book.

In San Giovanni Rotondo, Padre Alessio Parente, Capuchin, was a veritable Guardian Angel for me. He gave me time which he could ill afford, arranging interviews, acting as interpreter, translator, chauffeur, adviser, editor, quartermaster and most congenial, brotherly host. I was privileged to meet many of the friars of Padre Pio's Province, all of whom welcomed me with the warmth of Franciscan hospitality.

Many people, both Capuchins and laymen, from New York to Oklahoma, and from San Giovanni Rotondo to Sicily, told me how Padre Pio has helped them. I wish I could include all their stories. Maybe a second book on Padre Pio will do that.

I wish to thank the family of Father Dominic Meyer for sending me his fact-filled letters, and Mrs. Colette Kehoe for loaning me the precious letters which she had received from Maria Pyle.

I am deeply indebted to Monsignor Oreste Vighetti, the Vatican's Director of the Casa and International Director of the Padre Pio Prayer Groups, and to Miss Ida Lucibelli, for their invaluable assistance with source material especially on the Casa Sollievo.

When I returned from Italy, I had over forty hours of tapes to be translated into English. In that work, I received the precious help of Mrs. Harry Calandra, Miss Katherine Florio, Miss Anna Bavoso, Miss Loretta Moore, Miss Josephine Spirito, Mrs. Gabriela Palumbo, Mr. and Mrs. Richard Cacciato, Mrs. Ernest Ciaglia,

Michael Picarelli, Sister Emmanuel, O.P., Miss Edith Foss, and Victor Kelly. Father Capistran Ferrito, Capuchin, even came from New York to Oklahoma to help me with the translation of books and tapes. Mrs. Lucy Brooks helped me with the translation of Spanish source material.

Father Armand Dasseville, Capuchin, and especially Mrs. Rita Bisdorf, spent many, many hours editing my manuscript. Brother Giuseppe Pio (Brother Bill Martin, now Padre Giuseppe Pio, a Capuchin priest in Padre Pio's Province) sacrificed his precious time both in answering my questions and revising my manuscript.

I stand forever in debt to all the ladies who typed and retyped my manuscript: Mrs. Z. T. Helm, Mrs. Yvonne Perez, Mrs. Donna Sack, Mrs. Sera Barbaro, Mrs. Frances Peeples, Mrs. Frances Jacobson. Also I include my sister, Sister Mary Frances, C.S.A., and Miss Marie Kelly, a Third Order member at St. John the Baptist Church in New York City. I can never adequately thank Mrs. Lucille Greene for bearing the whole burden of love in retyping the entire manuscript.

At the head of this list I should have put Father Maurice Maurer, Capuchin, who struggled so patiently to teach me how to write when I was a high school student at St. Mary's Seminary, Garrison, N.Y.

May our beloved Padre Pio keep them all one with him in the love of the Sacred Hearts of Jesus and Mary.

In presenting this biography, the author declares his submission to the decree of Pope Urban VIII, the Law of the Church, and the decrees of the Holy See.

Rev. John Schug, Capuchin
St. Anne's Friary
Broken Arrow, Oklahoma

INTRODUCTION

Cleonice Morcaldi, a resident of San Giovanni Rotondo, made a white linen undershirt and gave it to her "Spiritual Father," Padre Pio. Three days later, he gave it back to her and asked her please to wash it.

She looked at it and gasped: "Madonna! It is one flagellation!" It was splattered with blood from top to bottom, from front to back.

Even today, few people realize that Padre Pio experienced the scourges of Christ on his back. But they were not his most conspicuous signs of conformity to Christ. What is more, he also bore the stigmata, the real and visible wounds of the crucifixion in his hands and feet and side.

How that happened can best be described in his own words. It was the morning of September 20, 1918. He was in the choir, as the Capuchins call their community chapel, making his thanksgiving after Mass.

"I was in the choir after the celebration of Holy Mass, when I was overcome with drowsiness as of a sweet sleep. All my internal and external senses, and also the faculties of my soul, experienced an indescribable quiet. . . . I discovered myself in front of a mysterious, exalted person (*personaggio*), similar to the person whom I saw on the evening of the 5th of August. The only difference was that this person was spilling blood from his hands and feet and heart. . . .

"The vision of the person faded away, and I noticed that my hands and feet and chest had been pierced and were bleeding profusely."

This man who encountered the crucified Christ was Padre Pio, a Capuchin priest in the small mountain town of San Giovanni Rotondo, in southern Italy. The story of his life is not a biography. It is an experience.

Just the externals of his life — his miracles, his stigmata (the five bleeding wounds of the crucifixion in his hands and feet and side), his bilocation (the ability to be in two places at one time), his gift of tongues (he could speak languages he never studied), his ability to read souls (he knew people's life stories without ever having met them), his crushing workload without a vacation or day off for fifty years — all of these were the bait which the Divine Fisherman used to hook hardened sinners and to convert Padre Pio's most skeptical and atheistic critics.

The accounts of these phenomena, while overwhelming, are easily enough verified and described. But to deal only with these externals would be to ignore a far greater phenomenon, the evolution of God's grace in the soul of this simple, lovable Capuchin friar. To come to know the *whole* man, body and soul, can make us stand before him with our mouths hanging open. The externals of his life pall into insignificance as we read his own unpretentious account, simple but sublime, of the evolution of his spiritual life of union with God, which he penned only under obedience to his spiritual director.

Awe-struck, we can look into his soul and hear him pour out his heart to Jesus on the Cross. We can share these prayers, for they were copied down during his ecstasies by his alert director, Padre Agostino.

No one can number the people whom this Wise Man of the Gargano led to God. In 1967, the United Press International estimated that a million-and-a-half persons visited him in that year alone. In 1968 the British Broadcasting Corporation filmed a documentary on him.

From morning to night people wanted to talk to him, laymen, priests, Bishops, Cardinals, doctors, politicians, young and old. From all over the world they pestered him with all kinds of questions, trivial and profound. "Should the family go to the shore this weekend?" "Should I take this job?" "Should I go to the hospital?" Yet, under all that pressure, he was always patient and composed. No issue, no matter how trivial, was unimportant to him. Whatever was important to his "spiritual children" was important to him.

His visitors did not always find him kind and gentle. Sometimes he seemed to be crude, almost ruthless. He called one man a pig and told him to get out of the confessional. But not a single case is known in which Padre Pio censured someone who didn't need it. In any given crowd, he knew whom to pat gently on the head and whom to growl at: "Get out of here, you sinner, until you really want to come back to God."

Padre Pio's mother and father:
Giuseppa and Grazio Forgione.
(Photo courtesy Casa Abresch)

Despite the intense pain of his five wounds, Padre Pio had a pleasant personality and a refined sense of humor. (Photo courtesy Casa Abresch)

DEDICATION

I dedicate this book to Our Lady of Grace, under whose mantle Padre Pio worked for fifty-two years in San Giovanni Rotondo.

CHAPTER 1

Enter the Gladiator

Almost from the year he was born Padre Pio was a gladiator. He battled with the devil and with God, with his parents, with his teachers, and with himself. His arena for nearly twenty years was Pietrelcina, not far from Naples, still a medieval town, where he was born on May 25, 1887. After that, his arena was in another town of southern Italy, San Giovanni Rotondo, just above the heel of the Italian boot, where he spent the last fifty-two years of his life.

He was baptized Francesco, a name chosen by his mother because of her deep devotion to St. Francis of Assisi. He was the second of eight children born to the poor peasant farmers Grazio and Giuseppa DeNunzio Forgione. Three of their children died in infancy. Michele, their first-born, spent several years working in Jamaica, N.Y. Felicita and Pellegrina died when they were about thirty. Grazia became a nun.

Francesco's father, Grazio, or Orazio, or Zi'Gra, was described by a friend as "basically a good man but not a saint." In his later years, Grazio recalled in his conversations with the Capuchins that as a baby Francesco was calm and quiet. But occasionally the child would try Grazio's patience with his loud and persistent crying. Grazio would respond with a string of colorful language against the baby.

On one occasion when Francesco would not stop crying, Grazio seized him and threw him onto the bed. The boy fell onto the floor. "Why has a little devil come into my house instead of a baby!" the father bellowed.

"You have killed my child!" his wife screamed. Francesco was not seriously hurt, but this fall cured him of his disturbing crying spells.

Among the reasons why he cried were his terrifying dreams. In recalling them to his spiritual director in later years he said: "As soon as my mother blew out the oil lamp, so many monsters stood near me that I cried. When she lit the lamp, I stopped crying, and the monsters disappeared. Then when she blew it out again, I started crying all over again because of the monsters."

These diabolical visions were counterbalanced by apparitions of the Blessed Virgin Mary and his Guardian Angel. But Francesco never thought that these apparitions were anything out of the ordinary. It was not until he was almost thirty years old that he even mentioned them to his spiritual director. "Don't *you* see Our Lady?" he asked Padre Agostino. When Padre Agostino said "No," Padre Pio said: "You are saying that out of humility." He called his Guardian Angel "the companion of my youth."

Nobody, not even Francesco, realized the work which God was accomplishing in him. To all appearances, he grew up as just another boy of Pietrelcina. The only observation which his friends made about him was hardly noteworthy, that he was rather quiet. He didn't care much to play with his friends. When he did play, his favorite sport was wrestling. His mother urged him to mix more with his friends, but he answered: "I don't like to play with them because they blaspheme."

A next door neighbor recalls how he and Francesco wrestled while their sheep grazed in the meadow nearby. They wrestled, he said, not because they were fighting, but to test their strength. "Once while wrestling," he said, "we fell down, and Francesco pinned my shoulders against the ground. I tried to roll over and reverse the situation, but it was useless. I started to use filthy language. Francesco immediately released his hold, got up and ran away. He absolutely never said any bad words, nor did he want to hear any."

Padre Pio described Vico Storto, the street on which he lived, as "a narrow little street, which looked like a monastery corridor where people could see each other and nearly shake hands from their windows." For about forty years this one-room adobe house in Pietrelcina was home for the whole Forgione family. Later on, his parents were able to buy another home on Vico Storto having two rooms, to serve as a bedroom and dining room for the children.

Down the street, at 1 Vico Storto, there was another one-room building which a mountain goat would have difficulty entering. It saddled a thirty-foot rock, which Padre Pio affectionately called "The *Morgia,* the Big Rock." Grazio bought this home after a stay in the United States. After Francesco became a Capuchin, he loved to use the *"Morgia"* to pray and study in. It was there that he spent most of his time between 1902 and 1916.

The family eked out their meager existence from a near-barren five acres of ground called "Piana Romana," a couple of miles from Pietrelcina. But this was barely enough for the survival of the family. Grazio wanted more for his children. He was especially anxious to have Francesco go to school. Francesco, from the time he was five years old, spoke about his desire to be a priest, and he dedicated himself to St. Francis of Assisi.

"If you learn quickly," his father admonished him,

"and are not like your brother, you will see that pappa will make a monk out of you."

A friend who had emigrated to Brazil wrote a letter to Grazio and told him: "You can see the golden tiles on the roofs of the palaces." So to earn money to send Francesco to school, Grazio packed a suitcase, and with the dream of making millions for his family, he left for Brazil.

Padre Pio liked to reminisce about his father's quixotic trip. "The poor villagers! When they landed, they looked up and were surprised to realize that the rooftops were just the same as those in their own Italian villages. They asked about the man who had given them the information, and they found him working like a slave in a restaurant kitchen."

Despondent at not being able to make his fortune, Grazio borrowed money and returned to Pietrelcina. The only money he had was that with which he had started. When he met his wife, he said: "Here is the money you gave me," and threw it at her.

In spite of Grazio's disappointment in Brazil, Francesco was able to begin his elementary schooling. His classes were taught by two farmers, Saginario and Scocca, two men of the town who could read and write. Classes were taught in a spare room of a house, without any desks.

Francesco tried to study, but his classmates pestered him. When he complained about them to his teachers, they gave him no sympathy. "Why don't you take a stick and break it over their heads?" He only answered: "Our Lord will take care of them."

Classes were held at night. During the day, the children led their sheep to graze in a pasture. On their way to the pasture, the children ate their breakfast, or they would save it until they arrived in the pasture.

With Francesco breakfast was a production. He would sit down, spread out the napkin over his knees, raise his eyes in prayer, and then begin to eat. If a crumb fell, he would pick it up and eat it. A friend who recalls these scenes from their childhood said that they did not consider Francesco eccentric, because "we called bread God's grace, and we were told never to waste it." But because Francesco ate from a white napkin, they dubbed him "The Gentleman."

After breakfast he put his books on his napkin and began to study. The rest of his friends played games. "We envied him," they confessed, "because we knew that we would never become more than peasants."

As modest as the family finances were, the Forgiones managed occasionally to take a day off. One day Grazio and Francesco went to a fiesta in the town of Altavilla Irpina, where there was a famous shrine to St. Pellegrino. As usual, they started their trip with the Sign of the Cross and the names of Jesus and Mary. At the fiesta they prayed awhile at the altar of the saint. Then his father said: "Franci, let's go home."

"Pa," he answered, "let's stay a little while longer." His father kept prodding him, but Francesco's answer was always the same.

Next to Francesco was a poor woman holding a sick and emaciated child, praying to St. Pellegrino for a miracle. Francesco was praying with her. Tired and desperate, the mother cursed the martyr and flung her child onto the altar. There was a moment of fearful silence, and then a cry of joy. The child stood up by himself, completely cured.

The news spread quickly. The bells rang out and the crowds flocked to the shrine. Grazio, who didn't know of his son's involvement in this, was squeezed like a sardine. He took out his frustration first on Francesco. "Stubborn!" he said. "You didn't want to come out when I told you. Now we will be pinned in here for God knows how long." Finally they elbowed their way to the door.

When Padre Pio recalled this story in later years,

tears welled up in his eyes. "During the return trip, my father gave a whack to the poor donkey, who wasn't responsible, but he only frowned at me, the one who was the cause of our being late."

Padre Pio insisted that it was God who worked the miracle through Saint Pellegrino, and not through himself. But Padre Raffaele, Padre Pio's confrere for about thirty years, adds this comment: "Who worked the miracle, St. Pellegrino or the future Padre Pio? My thoughts go back to the first miracle worked by Jesus at the wedding at Cana. There we have the mother, here we have the father. I think it is the first miracle worked by the child Padre Pio along with St. Pellegrino. It is proof that he prayed with more fervor than the mother herself, and let's say, with more simplicity and innocence."

When he was ten years old, Francesco became seriously ill, probably because of intestinal trouble. The doctor prescribed some pills, but Francesco didn't take them. His cure came not from medicine but from some peppers his mother had prepared for dinner. "I was in the next room," he recalled many years later, "and enjoyed smelling the peppers, but I absolutely dared not ask for them. After the meal was cooked, mother took half of the peppers out to the workers in the field and put the other half in the cupboard." Francesco made sure his mother was far away and struggled to his feet. He learned against the wall because of his weakness, went to the cupboard and filled his belly with them. He returned to bed and fell sound asleep.

When his mother returned she found him asleep, perspiring profusely, his face as red as the peppers he had eaten. Again she called the doctor. He found his temperature, heart and pulse normal. The doctor feared a relapse, but the peppers achieved a healthy cathartic effect and the boy felt perfectly well. He pestered his mother for permission to get out of bed and to go into the fields where the men were working, but she refused.

Giuseppa had work to do in the fields, so she asked a neighbor to look after Francesco. The boy took advantage of her absence, got dressed, and bolted out of the house before his baby sitter realized he was gone. The fresh country air was all he needed for perfect convalescence.

About this time Francesco had his first experience with smoking, which cured him for life. "I was about ten years old," he recalled, "when one day at Piana Romana my Uncle Pellegrino called me and said: 'Come here, Francesco, you are quick. Here's some money. Go to town and buy me a Toscano cigar and matches. Hurry!'"

Francesco bought the cigar and matches, but on the way back he sat down on a stone by a stream. He said to himself: "Let's see what it's like to smoke." He took one puff and fell over. The earth turned upside down. He was dizzy, but managed to return to the farm. He told the whole story to his uncle, who burst out laughing. He never tried to smoke after that.

When Saginario and Scocca had taken their class as far as they were able, Francesco continued his elementary schooling under Don Domenico Tizzani. This was an uphill struggle, not because of the studies but because of the teacher. Tizzani was an apostate priest, living in public concubinage with his wife and daughter. Francesco found it impossible to respect him as a teacher. The boy had his own values, which were totally at variance with those of Tizzani.

On his way to class, Francesco served daily Mass. This annoyed Tizzani. He told Giuseppa that her son had no brains for book learning and would be better off working in the fields. When Francesco heard that, he snapped back: "My head is no good? You mean that his head is no good. He is living in sin in his own house."

In later life he said about his teacher: "Don Domenico was a very clever teacher, kind and reserved, and never said a word of his pitiful affair to his pupils. He was often willing to break up his unhappy relationship, but there was always his daughter. He remained shut up at home and never dared to come out of doors for fear of being heckled. One day the Archbishop came to Pietrelcina and sent for him, but he excused himself. He wanted to go, but he dared not be seen in the street walking to the rectory, so he continued dragging his cursed chain indoors."

Shortly after Francesco was ordained a priest, he passed by Tizzani's home and saw that his daughter was very dejected. "How is your father?" he asked.

She answered: "He is very ill." The Padre asked if he could see him. No priest had ever dared to enter his home. Padre Pio entered, heard his confession, and in a few days Tizzani died at peace with God.

In the course of the school year, Tizzani raised his fee from two to five lire. (At present there are about 600 lire to a dollar!) Again the meager family budget could not bear the burden. Grazio decided: "I must go again to America." This time he went to "Little America," the United States, in 1907.

Grazio settled in New York City, in Jamaica, in St. Pius V Parish. Perhaps he headed there because his son Michele had previously lived nearby in Flushing, where he worked on the construction of the Post Office.

Grazio did so well that he was able to return to San Giovanni Rotondo for a visit. Then he returned to Jamaica and stayed until 1919. He had not intended to remain so long, but he was prevented from returning home by World War I. Padre Pio quipped about this trip: "Little America gave him something, but Big America (Brazil) gave him nothing."

While Grazio was in New York, he heard that Francesco was getting nowhere in his studies. Giuseppa had written to him: "Francesco makes no progress because he spends all his time in church. He goes to church in the morning, and in the evening he goes to church again, so he can't learn very much."

Giuseppa had reason to complain about the time Francesco spent in church. Often he would simply sit down in church and ask the sacristan not to tell anyone he was there. He went to Mass every morning, and stopped in for a visit again on his way home in the evening. En route he paused for a short prayer whenever he passed one of the votive shrines of Mary which flank the roadsides.

"What shall I write to your father?" Giuseppa remonstrated. "He has gone to America to keep you in school and make you a monk." Francesco listened in silence. Tears rolled down his cheeks. "Mamma," he sobbed, "it is not I who make no progress, and it is not the church that keeps me from learning. It is my teacher. He is a bad priest."

Giuseppa admitted to her husband that "the choice of the teacher was not a good one. What can he learn from an unfrocked priest?" Grazio wrote back to her: "Look for a better teacher."

She approached a layman, Angelo Caccavo, and asked him to tutor her son. She tried to speak politely and to choose the right words, but in her confusion she could only say: "Don Angelo, I entrust my brat (*bardascio*) to you!"

Caccavo at first refused, because he was a friend of Tizzani and didn't want to have a falling out with him. But Giuseppa and other relatives pressed him, and he finally accepted. She told him: "I hand him over to you. Beat him if necessary."

The two years which Francesco spent with Caccavo were profitable. He was a meticulous student. But they were far from the most enjoyable years of his life. His classmates often played tricks on their shy new classmate. One of the girls in his class wrote a passionate love note, and the boys stuck it into the pocket of Francesco's jacket. They then began coughing to draw the teacher's attention.

"What's wrong?" Caccavo asked.

"Francesco!"

"What about him?"

"Francesco is making love."

"Is that true?" he asked Francesco.

"It is not true," Francesco answered. Meanwhile the boys were pointing to his pocket.

"Don't lie."

"I'm telling the truth."

"I warn you that I'll beat you."

"Do as you please. I've done nothing."

Caccavo searched his jacket and found the love note.

"What of your becoming a monk? You are a liar." And he began to beat Francesco. The boy tried to hide under the desk but could not escape a severe beating.

The next day the girl confessed to the teacher. He kicked her down the stairs.

Many years later, Padre Pio recalled: "Poor Caccavo, how sorry he was then, but nobody could erase the black and blue marks he had given me."

Although his classmates used Francesco as the butt of their practical jokes, they relied on him when they needed a spokesman, especially when they were looking for favors. On one occasion the school had a two-day holiday, but the boys complained that they would spend all their time traveling. They asked Francesco to get another day of vacation. In his shyness he hesitated to ask, but he spoke up and was given the extra day for them.

While Francesco was studying under Caccavo, the whole family worked as a team so he could have time to study. His father was in the United States. His mother and sisters worked in the fields at Piana Romana. When Francesco was not in class, he would remain home and study. His mother left a cooked meal for him, and Francesco helped himself to it.

One day his mother left an elaborate lunch of *zucchini alla parmigiana* and grapes. Francesco pushed the *zucchini* aside as though it were poison and ate only the grapes. Later when his mother saw this, she cried. Many years afterwards, Padre Pio recalled: "If only I had thought that mother would be so hurt, I'd have swallowed all the *zucchini*, but unfortunately, I became aware of it only when she burst out crying."

His friends kept trying to lure him away from his studies to play games with them. But he always told them: "Later — later on."

With his father in New York, and his mother and sisters at Piana Romana, Francesco was not always a paragon of obedience. He was not selfish or sneaky, but if he had his mind made up to do something, he let nothing stand in his way. He wanted to make a pilgrimage with his school to Our Lady's shrine at Pompeii. He knew he would never get permission from his mother. So he simply made the decision on his own.

When Grazio heard about the trip, he wrote a stern letter to Giuseppa. She read the letter to Francesco, and Francesco wrote back to his father: "You are quite right in complaining to mother about my trip to Pompeii. However, you must know that next year, God willing, all holidays and pleasures will end, because I shall leave here to follow a better life. It's true, I spent a little money, but now I promise to earn it by studying."

We get a beautiful insight into the working of Francesco's mind as a child from an essay he wrote when he was about ten years old. It is entitled: *If I Were King*.

> "Oh, if I were king! What beautiful things I'd like to do. First of all, I would always be a religious king, as I am now and hope always to be. Above all I would fight divorce, which many wicked people long for, and I would have the Sacrament of Matrimony better observed.

"Look at what became of Julian the Apostate, who was brave, temperate and studious. He made the great mistake of denying Christianity in which he had been brought up. He had already intended to revive paganism. He only wasted his time, because he received the odious name of Apostate. I, on the contrary, would try to make my name famous by always beating the path of a true Christian, and woe to those who would not choose to follow it! I would punish them immediately either by imprisoning them or by punishing or putting them to death. I would have as a rule the command of Alexander Severus: 'Treat other people as you would like to be treated.'

"During my reign I would often visit the provinces in order to improve their administration, and I would leave memorials everywhere and build beautiful monuments such as gates, roads, circuses, libraries, statues, theaters and other things. I would be friendly, kind, and law-abiding. I'd go about like an ordinary man, listen to everybody and dress plainly, wearing clothes made by women at home. All the greatest writers would be welcome at my Court and all the masters of rhetoric would get good salaries. I would promote the arts and follow Vespasian's precept: 'Only a friend of mankind is worthy to rule.' "

CHAPTER 2

Fra Pio

Francesco reached a turning point in his life when he was about fifteen. He had often spoken to his parents, his parish priest Don Salvatore Pannullo, and his Uncle Pellegrino, about his desire to become a priest. His choice was strongly influenced by the Capuchin Brother Camillo.

The Capuchins are one of the three branches of the Franciscan Order. They were established in Italy in 1528 as an independent group of Franciscans, to restore the original interpretation of the Rule written in 1209 by St. Francis of Assisi.

Today, almost 13,000 Capuchins form the fourth largest Order of priests and Brothers in the world. Capuchins are not monks. A monk is a man who is permanently assigned to his religious house. All Franciscans, including Capuchins, are friars. Literally, that means "Brothers." St. Francis wanted to found a brotherhood, not a monastic group of monks. Even Francesco's parents apparently did not realize the distinction between a monk and a friar. Capuchins seldom correct a misinformed person. There are more important issues to occupy our minds.

When Padre Pio was a young man, the Capuchins still had the "quest." That is, they went out begging with a sack over their backs. Brother Camillo, who was stationed at the Capuchin novitiate house in Morcone, quested in Pietrelcina.

Francesco became very fond of him, with his brown habit, white cord, bare feet and sandals, and especially his beard. The Capuchin beard is a rarity in religious Orders. From the time of the Order's establishment, it has been a unique trademark of the Capuchin-Franciscans. No other Franciscan group wears the beard.

His Uncle Pelligrino offered to help Francesco to join the Capuchin Order and wrote to the Father Provincial in Foggia. But the novitiate house, the stage in the formation program after high school, was full. The Father Provincial said that Francesco would have to wait.

Pellegrino could see no reason to wait, and he urged Francesco to join another religious Order at Montevirgine, where he said the religious lived much better. But Francesco responded immediately: "No, I don't want that, because they have no beards."

Then Pellegrino tried to convince him to join a community at Sant' Angelo a Capolo. Again he insisted that Francesco should join a group which lives a better life than that of the Capuchins.

Francesco's only question was: "Do they have beards?" The answer was negative. Again Francesco's pat answer: "Then I say no."

Pellegrino began to lose patience and recommended another branch of the Franciscan Order "who are not like the friars at Morcone, who look like so many consumptives." He growled at Francesco: "Stop all this talk about a beard." In later years Padre Pio recalled: "I had a fixed idea about Brother Camillo's beard, and nobody could cool my enthusiasm."

After a couple of months, a letter of acceptance came from the Provincial. But there was another hurdle to clear. Just before Francesco was supposed to leave for Morcone, an envious altar boy wrote an anonymous letter to Don Pannullo, Francesco's pastor in Pietrelcina, accusing Francesco of making love to the daughter of the stationmaster of Pietrelcina. Francesco didn't even know the girl.

The letter was delivered to Don Pannullo shortly before Francesco was due to leave for Morcone. Don Pannullo discussed the letter with the other parish priests, but he told Francesco nothing about it. Without any explanation, Don Pannullo debarred Francesco from all religious services. He could not serve Mass, he could not wear a surplice, he could not even go near the sacristy.

Meanwhile, Don Pannullo appointed a priest to spy on Francesco to see if he should ever meet the girl. Francesco searched his mind for a reason to understand the priest's change of attitude. He could only conclude: "It must be the custom before someone joins the friars."

About a month passed. Finally the priest, through handwriting analysis, discovered the culprit and the boy confessed.

Although Padre Pio never forgot this incident, he held no grudge against the boy. He told his spiritual director: "I prayed for those who slandered me and I will continue to pray for them. The most I ever said was an occasional: 'Lord, if a whipping is necessary to convert them, give it to them, but only if it will do them some good.'"

Just before he entered the friary he became very weak. He was examined by a doctor, who feared that he might have tuberculosis. The tests showed no signs of tuberculosis, but they did indicate his susceptibility to bronchial inflammation. Sixty-five years later this would be the immediate cause of his death.

It was at this time that he experienced a vision, a prelude to his lifelong battle with the devil. He had just received Holy Communion and seemed to be in a huge and magnificent hall. On one side were many beautiful people. On the opposite side were people with hideous faces. Francesco was in the middle. Jesus appeared to him and took him by the arm. A huge monster came from the end of the hall to devour him, but Our Lord comforted him. When the monster approached him, it was struck down by a bolt of lightning and disappeared with a horrible yell. Jesus said to Francesco: "That is the fiend against whom you will have to fight." The vision disappeared.

He apparently experienced another vision around this time, when he and some other boys were out for a walk with Don Pannullo. Suddenly he stopped and said: "What a beautiful aroma. I smell incense and hear the chanting of friars." He pointed to the exact spot where a Capuchin house and church would be built. This prophecy was fulfilled in 1928, when the cornerstone of a friary and church was blessed by Luigi Cardinal Lavitrano.

Just before he left for Morcone on January 6, 1903, Francesco asked his mother's blessing. She said: "My dear child, my heart is bleeding, but St. Francis calls you, and you must go."

His father at this time was in America. Francesco wrote to him: "Don't worry about my brother. He does his duty and is always kind to mother. The same is true of my sisters. My mother and brother always look after them."

He was given the Franciscan habit at Morcone on January 22, at the age of fifteen. Also he was given the name of Pio, after St. Pope Pius V. Until his ordination to the priesthood he would be called Fra (Brother) Pio.

On January 22, 1903, he was invested as a novice at the Capuchin friary in Morcone. This began his period of spiritual formation, but without any obligation to remain in the Order. Now he was a Capuchin, living the Franciscan life to the full, including, at last, a beard.

He received the traditional brown robes of the Order,

with sandals and a thin white rope for a belt. He also received the "*cappuccio*," the cowl, the hood. The Capuchin cowl is so distinctive that the children of Camerino, where the Order began, nicknamed the new group "*Cappuccini*, people wearing an unusual hood."

A year later he made his first legal but temporary commitment to God, vowing along with his classmates to live for three years in poverty, chastity, and obedience according to the Rule of St. Francis of Assisi. During these three years, he pursued the usual seminary studies for the priesthood on a college level with a major in philosophy.

This period of his "simple vows" as they are called was marked with a return of his original weak physical condition. Sometimes, without any apparent reason, he would run up a fever of 125 degrees Fahrenheit (52 degrees Centigrade). "No ordinary thermometer," said Padre Michaelangelo, a Capuchin who lived with him, "could measure Padre Pio's temperature. A bathroom thermometer was necessary. I was present once when the doctor wanted to take his temperature, but Fra Pio said, 'No, the thermometer will break! But the doctor wanted his thermometer to be broken by Pio, so he gave it to him. In an instant, 'Bang!' the mercury shot up and broke it immediately. It could not even measure his temperature."

What did these high fevers mean? One doctor asked him the reason for his high temperatures. Padre Pio answered him: "You are the doctor. You tell me."

Padre Michaelangelo considered the high fevers as an external sign of Fra Pio's suffering. Maybe, but does that explain them? The doctor had no explanation, we can only guess.

Maybe Padre Pio did give us an explanation. He often wrote about "a fire which burns my whole being." He wrote about "a mysterious fire which I felt from my heart, which I couldn't understand." The fire was so real to him, as he said, that "I felt the need to put ice on it to extinguish this fire which is consuming me."

In later years, Dr. Cardone recalled how he examined Fra Pio soon after his novitiate year. "Doctors," he said, "had diagnosed pulmonary tuberculosis and had prognosticated not more than a few months of life. But when I examined him, I came quickly and correctly to a contrary opinion. Yes, he was frail and thoroughly run-down because of his fasting, insomnia, his ascetical and penitential practices and the still active bronchitis which he had contracted in the country, in the hovel at Piana Romana where he went to pray.

"But that is quite a different story having nothing to do with tuberculosis. So much so that after the tuberculin injections, the reactions were always negative. If I had been dealing with tuberculosis, we would not be talking about him now. Together with his uncle I even took him for consultation to Naples, to Professor Castellino, a very famous doctor at the time, and he, too, eliminated the tubercular nature of the illness."

For three years Dr. Cardone treated Fra Pio. "He had become run-down," the doctor said, "and I treated him. Then he recovered and went back to his monastery." The doctor stated that during those examinations Fra Pio "looked as normal as any other Brother and without any peculiarities."

In 1907, Fra Pio pronounced his solemn vows, his final, permanent commitment to God as a Capuchin. "I, Fra Pio, vow and promise to almighty God, to the Blessed Virgin Mary, to our holy Father St. Francis, to all the saints, and to you, Father, to observe all the days of my life, the Rule of the Friars Minor, confirmed by Pope Honorius, living in obedience, without property, and in chastity." Although he had never doubted his own mind, he now had the reassurance of the Church that he was where he belonged. He took the plunge with a song in his heart and never regretted it.

After his profession of final vows, he went to the house of studies at San Marco la Catola, where he completed his course of philosophy.

From there he went to Serracapriola, in the Province of Foggia, to begin his four-year course of theology. One of his professors was Padre Agostino, who later became his spiritual director and the source of an abundance of information on Padre Pio's whole life.

But again ill health set in and his superiors gave him a leave of absence with his family in Pietrelcina. For about seven years before and after his ordination to the priesthood, Fra Pio shuttled between the monastery and his parents' home. While at home, he was tutored by his old friend Don Pannullo.

CHAPTER 3

Padre Pio

Fra Pio was ordained to the priesthood in the chapel of the Archbishop of Benevento, on Friday, August 10, 1910. From that time on, he was known as Padre Pio. We will resist the temptation to sermonize on his ordination, an echo in time of the eternal call by which the Father conformed him to the ministry of His Son, Jesus Christ. We will simply mention that Padre Pio's mother Giuseppa attended the ceremony, along with his brother and sisters. His father was still in New York, unable to afford another journey home.

From the time of his ordination, Giuseppa never again called her son Francesco. He was always Padre Pio. She insisted on kissing his hand, a custom still universal in southern Italy. He would try to stop her, but always she managed to grasp his hand before he could pull it away.

"First," she would say, "I kiss your hand for Aunt Libra (the first kiss), and for Aunt Pellegrina (second kiss), for Aunt Philomena," (third kiss) and so on for a dozen aunts and godmothers. And at the end she would say: "And now, Padre Pio, I kiss your hand for myself."

At this point he stopped her. Throwing his hands up in the air he would say: "What is this? The son should kiss the hand of the mother and not the mother the hand of the son."

Instinctively, we reach for nice things to say about so reverent an occasion. However, we will probably never be able to add much to these meager details of his ordination. But there is no need for dismay. From that year onward, all that Padre Pio did, all that was done to him, provided more grist than any writer's mill could grind in a lifetime.

Until Padre Pio was ordained a priest, his life was a symphony, simple in its arrangement, pleasant to listen to. But between his ordination in 1910 and his death in 1968, the symphony took on a Wagnerian complexity. He hungered for God, but being convinced of his own uselessness and unworthiness before God, he pleaded for death as a relief from this agony.

So rapt was he in prayer that at the beginning of his priestly life his Mass lasted almost three hours. The people, however, complained of this and called him "a crazy monk."

He saw and talked with his Guardian Angel, but lurid temptations and obsession by the devil often left him bruised and bleeding.

As early as 1910, the stigmata, the wounds of Christ crucified, appeared visibly on his body, but even these were to prove a source of embarrassment and confusion to him.

"I feel crushed, dear Father," he wrote to his spiritual director, "and can find no place to hide. I am sick and sick at heart. I cannot go on any longer. The thread seems as though it must surely break from one moment to the next, but this moment never arrives."

Shortly after his ordination, Padre Pio was sent to study Sacred Eloquence under Padre Agostino. Then his health again began to bother him. He could not celebrate

Mass. For twenty-one days he ate nothing except Holy Communion. Accompanied by his superior, he visited doctors in Naples, but they could make very little or nothing of his illness.

After several weeks, to everyone's amazement, he regained good health and went to Pietrelcina. With few exceptions, he remained there until 1916. The apparent external reason for going to Pietrelcina was his health, but the real motive will never be known. He said: "I would be lacking charity if I would tell you why the Lord wanted me at Pietrelcina."

At Venafro, few people detected the divine alchemy which was transforming the body and soul of the young Capuchin friar. But one man did know, Padre Agostino, his Provincial Superior and later his spiritual director. He began to keep a diary on Padre Pio. Among his entries he wrote:

"In November, 1911, Padre Evangelista (the superior) and I noticed the first supernatural phenomena. We were present several times when he went into ecstasy and many times when he was assaulted by the devil. I wrote down everything that I heard from his mouth during those ecstasies and how the assaults of Satan happened. At Venafro and at Pietrelcina, I was present at several ecstasies in which Jesus, the Madonna, and his Guardian Angel appeared to him. The ecstasies lasted an hour and even more. He had visions of the seraphic Father Saint Francis. The heavenly visions were usually preceded by diabolical ones. Satan appeared to him in the form of a fierce beast, of a man, of a woman, of a Brother. Sometimes the devil took the form of St. Francis, of the Madonna, of a crucifix. Padre Pio soon discovered the diabolical trick by invoking the most holy name of Jesus. After the diabolical apparitions, Padre Pio went into ecstasy, with the visions of the Lord, of the Madonna, of the saints, and of his Guardian Angel, who was never absent."

The shrewd Padre Agostino not only chronicled his own observations but also dutifully copied down whatever he heard Padre Pio speak in ecstasy. For an hour or two, repeatedly in the course of a day, Padre Pio would lose consciousness of everything and everybody around him.

The original Italian of Padre Pio's prayers is sublime. They are part of the *Diario*, the diary of Padre Agostino, which has been published by the Capuchins at San Giovanni Rotondo.

Eavesdropping on an ecstasy of December 12, 1911, Padre Agostino transcribed this prayer of Padre Pio:

> "My Jesus, how beautiful you seem to me this morning . . . but tell me, my Lord, are you in my heart? Did I receive you this morning? Yes? . . . And who gave me Communion? . . . My Father? . . . He always gives me Communion! . . . If I ask him he always replies: 'I gave you the Blessed Sacrament with these unworthy hands' . . . But my Jesus, do I have to ask him? . . . Will you tell me the truth? . . . I know you do not lie. . . . Are you saying yes with your own mouth? . . . But Jesus, what sign do you give me? . . . Who called me? . . . He called! Was I asleep? What did he say to me? . . . 'Pio, do you see Jesus in my unworthy hands!' . . . Ah my Jesus, pardon me. I already feel you in my heart as the disciples did at Emmaus . . . I feel you. . . . With all your kindness . . . I no longer thirst for you. . . . Ah my dear Jesus. . . . How can I live without you? . . . Come often, my Jesus. . . . You alone can possess my heart. . . . If I had all the hearts in the world I would offer them to you. . . . My sweet Jesus, my love for you keeps me going. . . . Thank you. . . . Goodbye."

Padre Agostino also recorded a second prayer of Padre Pio on the same day:

"My Jesus, why do you seem so very young this morning? You have become so small. My Guardian Angel, do you see Jesus? . . . Well then, bow to Him. . . . That is not enough. . . . Kiss His wounds. . . . Good? . . . My good little Guardian Angel! . . . You are so serious. . . . What must I call you? . . . What is your name? . . . Oh, my Angel, I beg your pardon. Bless Jesus for me. . . . My Jesus, oh, my Jesus, why are you so small? . . . But tell me. . . . Come closer to me. . . . Tell me, can you speak? . . . You are so small. . . . Tell me, Jesus, did I receive Communion this morning? Yes? . . . Who gave it to me? . . . Ah, it is always he! . . . If I ask him he always tells me the same story: 'I gave you Communion myself!' . . . And he even speaks French: *Petit Enfant, . . . Petit Enfant!* . . . But my Jesus, . . . What sign are you giving me? He called me. . . . But why was I asleep? . . . I was speaking to you! . . . And what did he say to me? He ordered me. . . . But how did he say it? . . . 'Pio, do you see Jesus? I command you in the name of this Jesus Whom I hold in my hands to receive Communion! . . . Oh yes, my Jesus. . . . Is there another sign? There was also the Guardian Angel who held out the little plate. Oh thank you, my Jesus! Thank you! Go to your own place now, my Jesus!

"Ah, my little Mother (*Mammina*), . . . My beautiful little Mother! . . . Oh how beautiful your eyes are. . . . You were right, Jesus. . . . Yes, you are beautiful. . . . If there were no Faith, then men would proclaim you a goddess. . . . Your eyes shine even brighter than the sun.

... You are so beautiful, my little Mother. I offer you glory, I love you, help me. ... If it is the will of God that I go there, then comfort me my dear little Mother.

"My Jesus ... there is no more time. ... Goodbye. ... I want to see you up there. ... What can heaven be like if it can be this good on earth. Goodbye, my sweet Jesus. Goodbye. ... Your love sustains me. ... *Arivederci!* Goodbye!"

A person might even be led to study Italian if for no other reason than to read the whole *Diario*. But it is only one of the tools we have to plumb the depth of Padre Pio's spirituality. The Capuchins at San Giovanni Rotondo have also published the *Epistolario,* a 1,377-page book consisting mainly of Padre Pio's letters to and from his spiritual directors, including a 176-page introductory biography and an appendix showing copies of some of Padre Pio's letters.

By commanding him under obedience, Padre Pio's spiritual directors extorted from him a description of the inner sanctum of his soul. As with the prayers which Padre Agostino copied down, the letters in the *Epistolario* need a poet and a philological genius to capture their grandeur. But again our humble translations will have to suffice.

Until 1922, although Padre Agostino was very close to Padre Pio, Padre Benedetto was his spiritual director. Padre Pio corresponded frequently with both priests. On one occasion he wrote to Padre Benedetto:

"That which hurts me most, dear Father, is the thought of Jesus in the Blessed Sacrament. My heart feels itself being attracted by a superior force before it unites itself to Him in the morning in Holy Communion. I hunger and thirst so much before receiving Him that I almost die of anxiousness, especially when I cannot unite myself with Him because of ill health. I am forced to go and eat His flesh. This hunger and thirst keep increasing more and more, rather than remaining satisfied after I have received Him in the Sacrament.''

In these letters we have the touchstone of the man's authenticity, his passion for Jesus in the Blessed Sacrament. This was the core of his personal spirituality and the driving force of his ministry.

"What is this fire which burns my whole being? Father mine, if Jesus makes us so happy on earth what will heaven be like? Sometimes I ask myself if there are people who do not feel their breasts burned by the divine fire. . . . This seems impossible to me especially if they are priests or religious. Perhaps they say they do not feel this fire because their hearts are bigger than mine. Only with this benign interpretation will I associate with them, so as not to charge them with being shameful deceivers.''

On April 18, 1912, he penned another letter which reveals his intimacy with God:

"At the end of Mass I stayed awhile with Jesus to give thanks. Oh, how sweet was the conversation with paradise this morning. Even if I should try to tell you all about it, I could not. There were things that cannot be translated into human language without losing their profound heavenly sense. There were no longer two hearts which beat, but only one. Mine had vanished like a drop of water which vanishes into the sea. Jesus was its paradise, its king. My joy was so intense and deep that I could no longer contain myself. Tears bathed my face. Yes, Father, when paradise floods into a heart, man cannot understand that this afflicted, exiled, weak and mortal heart cannot bear it without weeping. Yes, I repeat, only joy filled my heart, and it was this which made me weep for so long. Long live the Divine Prisoner!''

When we earthlings read such letters, we might envy him — until we learn the price he had to pay. In his own words, his sufferings were comparable "to that which the martyrs experienced when burned alive or brutally put to death when giving witness to their faith in Jesus Christ."

"Some people," he wrote, "will consider this comparison exaggerated, but I know what I am saying. For such incredulous people, I would like to ask the bountiful God to give them first-hand experience of this."

The martyrdom of which he speaks was caused by his desire to be with God, and, on the other hand, his realization of his nothingness before God. "If I knew I were of some value by remaining in this life, I would resign myself to go on supporting the burden that it brings me. But I have fear, and my fear is well grounded, that I may not fulfill my priestly ministry and therefore render useless the grace given me by the Bishop's laying on of hands in priestly ordination."

The only liberation from this which he could imagine was death. "By the depth of the compassion of God incarnate," he pleaded with Raffaelina, a spiritual daughter, "force yourself to ask the Spouse of Souls to break the chains that hold me in this body. If you do not, you will make yourself my assassin. I would be left alone in praying for this, and my prayer will never be answered."

One breath of relief given to him was familiarity with his Guardian Angel. "These persons from heaven," he wrote to Padre Agostino, "continually visit me." He called his Guardian Angel "the constant companion of my youth."

His Angel was a runner to and from the throne of God. When his spiritual children asked how they could contact him, Padre Pio usually told them: "Send your Guardian Angel." Occasionally people would ask if he had received a message sent by their Guardian Angel. "Do you think he is unfaithful like you?" he would respond.

When Father Dominic Meyer first went to San Giovanni Rotondo, he considered such statements to be flights of fancy. Father Dominic was a Capuchin priest, a professor of Dogmatic Theology, who became Padre Pio's personal English secretary. But after getting to know Padre Pio and meeting person after person whose messages by angelic telepathy were confirmed by subsequent events, he became a believer. He didn't hesitate to repeat a tongue-in-cheek complaint by Padre Pio. Father Dominic said to him one day: "Padre, you look tired. Didn't you sleep well last night?" The Padre replied: "The Guardian Angels kept me up all night with one message after the other."

A Royal Air Force officer wrote to Father Dominic: "Would you please, Father, thank Padre Pio for helping me on my journey home? On Sunday, April 16, I was halfway between Avignon and Lyons, France, and I had been walking all day and was very tired. I asked my Guardian Angel to ask Padre Pio to help me, and within ten minutes I got a car ride all the way back to Paris. Again, when I got there I had only fifty or sixty lire, and I tried to sell my watch to get some money to buy a ticket to Calais and to have a good meal. Again I sent my Guardian Angel to Padre Pio to help me get a good price for my watch. Inside of fifteen minutes I received a gift of 2,000 francs and was told to put it into a Catholic charity in England when I could afford it. Padre Pio certainly answers requests to the full. I still have my watch. Please thank him for me, Father."

When I hear similar stories told by the hundreds, stories told by responsible and sensible people, I become inclined to attribute some substance to them.

His Guardian Angel was not only the constant companion of his youth. His Angel also dictated letters for him in French and read the letters from Padre Agostino which were written in French.

Padre Pio never studied Greek or French, but occasionally he wrote to his spiritual director in those languages. The first time this happened, Padre Agostino expressed astonishment at receiving a letter in French and asked Padre Pio who had taught him the language. Padre Pio quipped: "As to your question about my knowledge of French, I answer with Jeremiah: 'A-a-a- I don't know how to talk.' "

Padre Agostino was not naïve, but he accepted Padre Pio's explanation. He wrote: "The Padre knows neither Greek nor French. His Guardian Angel explains it all, and the Padre answers me perfectly."

Don Pannullo, too, Padre Pio's parish priest in Pietrelcina, was curious about his gift of tongues. He wrote: "I questioned Padre Pio on how he could read and understand Greek without even knowing the alphabet, and he answered: 'You know, my Guardian Angel explains everything to me.' "

With a touch of humor, Padre Pio wrote a letter to Padre Agostino on September 20, 1912: "If the mission of the Guardian Angels is great, my own Guardian Angel certainly has a greater mission, because he has the job of being my interpreter of foreign languages, too."

His letters in French infuriated the devil. We know of nothing like that in the two thousand years of Church history. He never explained why, but we have documentary proof that in fact the devil did become enraged. Filthy smears of ink mysteriously appeared on the letters exchanged between Padre Pio and Padre Agostino. We can see with our own eyes a copy of one of these letters in the appendix of the *Epistolario*.

Padre Pio described one such incident in a letter to Padre Agostino, dated November 18, 1912:

"(Don Pannullo) knows about our battle with the devil. He suggested that I be near him when I opened your next letter. I did that, but when we opened the letter we found it all smeared with ink. Could this be the vendetta of Barbablu? I can never believe that you sent such a letter to me, because you know well of my blindness. In the beginning, the letter seemed to be illegible to both of us, but we placed a crucifix behind it and a little light came through, and we could read the letter, although with difficulty.''

Mention of Padre Pio's battles with the devils might elicit a patronizing snicker from an enlightened skeptic. One is free to mock his claim of seeing our Blessed Lord, the Virgin Mary, the Angels and the saints. One is free to propose the unreasonable hypothesis that Padre Agostino sent his letters already smeared with ink. But how explain away the physical poundings that he took, assaults which left him black and blue and once led his confreres to think that an earthquake had hit the house?

"The other night," he wrote on June 28, 1912, "was most horrifying. From 10:00 p.m. when I went to bed until about 5:00 in the morning the ugly thing kept beating me." This beating left him bleeding from the mouth.

"They jumped on me," he wrote on another occasion, "hurled me to the ground, beat me most mercilessly, and threw pillows, books and chairs up in the air and screamed the most filthy words."

Padre Pio found it repugnant to talk about these assaults. He did so only under obedience. But obedience itself became the cause of a more fierce attack. On October 14, 1912, he wrote to Padre Agostino:

"The devil at once began suggesting to me: 'You would please Jesus a lot more if you broke off all relations with your Father. He is a very dangerous person for you, and he is the cause of great distraction for you. Time is precious. Do not waste it in this dangerous correspondence with him. Spend this precious time in praying for your health, which is in great danger.' "

Padre Pio told Padre Agostino how he handled that temptation: "I answered him in an evidently sarcastic way. I told him that I confessed my error, that I had been under a false impression. I told him that I did not believe that you were very clever as a spiritual director.

"This was certainly some answer for them — I say them, because there was more than one, although only one spoke — because they threw themselves upon me, cursing me and threatening to destroy me if I didn't decide to change my mind about keeping in touch with you.

"This is the war which even today is waged against me. The devil absolutely demands that I cut off all relations and communication with you. And he threatens me that, if I insist on refusing to listen to him, he will do things to me that the human mind could never picture."

On and on the battle raged. Again he wrote to his spiritual director:

"The struggle with hell has reached the point where it can no longer continue. The ship of my soul is about to be overwhelmed by the ocean waves. My Father, really I can go on no longer. I feel the ground giving way under my feet. My forces fail me. I die and taste all deaths together in every moment of my life.

"The enemy is very strong and, all things considered, it seems that victory favors the enemy. Poor me, who will save me from the hands of such a strong, powerful enemy who doesn't leave me alone for an instant, either by day or by night?

"Is it ever possible that the Lord will let me fall? Unfortunately, I deserve it, but can it be true that the goodness of our heavenly Father must be defeated by my evil? Never, dear Father. Once again I feel love for my Lord rising like a giant in my poor heart. Once again I feel Faith and the strength to shout aloud with St. Peter: 'Lord save me, for I am perishing.' "

Were it not for such pathos and the magnificence of his letters, Padre Pio's incessant pleas for relief would be tedious. Seven months later he is still repeating the same agonizing theme:

"Always darkness and thorns, my Father. Some ray of light, some drop of comfort from your letters, and then fall the shadows, even more bitter than thorns.

"A continuous storm overwhelms me, and if there is a fleeting momentary lull, it is never any longer than for me to say a Hail Mary. I curl up within myself in fear and trembling with a question on my lips: What will happen to me now?

"I certainly know that I feel a burning thirst to suffer greatly, and I feel a continuous need to keep saying to the Lord: 'Either to suffer or to die.' Indeed, 'Always to suffer and never to die.'

"But such an ardent desire to suffer, dear Father, makes me fear that it doesn't come from God, because nature rebels and flees from suffering when it is put to the test, even though the desire to suffer persists. My desire to suffer opposes the dictates of my reason and the inspirations of grace. This is the cause of the martyrdom which is tearing my soul apart. I feel united with God through my spirit and through my will. At the same time my flesh and nature, which are always discontented, would detach themselves from the cross and the will of God.

"Can it be true that the Lord has finally sent this desolation which I now experience? Has He answered my entreaties by the grace of letting me always suffer and participate in the sufferings of the Divine Master? In your last letter you assured me that this is so. I cannot begin to imagine that my present condition is a grace. It seems to me to be a punishment from heaven which I justly deserve.

"I know that no one is spotless before God, but my deformity is inconceivable to the human mind. God has torn aside the veil which has hidden my uncleanness. He has finally revealed before my eyes all my hidden failings and I can see that my deformity is so great that my very clothes shudder in horror at my uncleanness.

"How then can I help but think of this when this distorted picture is always before me? My accuser is not a man to whom I can easily excuse my behavior, but God, a judge from whom there is no appeal, and no advocate can stand between me and Him. But my God, may He not take His mercy from me.''

Throughout this unending carnage, Padre Pio's visions of Jesus did not offer him any relief. They only added fuel to the fire, because they let him see his own nothingness in the light of the Light of the World. "It is true," he wrote, "that my prayers are more worthy of punishment than reward, because I have completely disgusted Jesus with my countless sins.''

Padre Agostino thought that Padre Pio's battle with the devil lasted only for eight years, from 1910 to 1918, when he said the devil was conquered. He may be correct, if he refers to the devil's assaults on Padre Pio almost daily. But Barbablu was not yet conquered. The physical beatings continued, although only sporadically, until he was an old man in his eighties. Nor did the other obsessions by the devil stop. They got worse.

On one hot summer night in S. Elia Pianisi, Padre Pio could not sleep. He heard someone walking up and down in the room next door. Thinking it was Fra Anastasio, he went to the window to exchange a few words with him. Sitting on the window sill of the next room was a monstrous black dog, staring at him with wild fiery eyes. Before Padre Pio could cry out, the creature took a tremendous leap and vanished over the housetop. Only later did he learn that Anastasio had moved to a different room and that his room had been empty that night.

Frequently while he was in his room he found himself surrounded by hideous monsters who jeered at him and challenged him to fight them. One of these devils appeared as Padre Agostino, and urged him to give up his life of penance and striving for perfection. The devil assured him that God didn't approve of his way of life. Padre Pio saw through the trick and cried out: *"Viva Gesu!"* and the apparition vanished.

In Pietrelcina, claw marks and ink stains which the

devil left on the walls can still be seen. In the Capuchin friaries in which Padre Pio was stationed, books in his room were thrown around and torn, blankets were strewn on the floor. Chairs were heard being dragged around, and ink was splattered all over the walls. Throughout his entire life, the devil continued to appear to him in the form of wild animals or naked women.

During the few months he spent at the Friary of St. Anne, in Foggia, the chaos caused by the devil became so unbearable that the community wanted him transferred. His local superior went into his room and said: "Padre Pio, I'm going to stay here until I see just what is going on!"

Padre Pio pleaded: "Father Guardian, I recommend for the good of your soul that you leave immediately."

Occasionally the devil's attacks were prompted by revenge against Padre Pio for an exorcism. An exorcism is a blessing of the Church by which the devil is cast out.

In July, 1964, a woman possessed by the devil was brought to San Giovanni Rotondo to be exorcised. She spoke in an unnaturally deep, booming, bass voice.

When she saw Padre Pio, she roared: "Pio, we will see you tonight." The people in the church paid no attention to her, thinking that she was mentally deranged, talking that way to a priest. That night, not the woman but the devils in her kept their promise. What must have been the force of their attack! The walls of the 350-year-old friary are solid masonry two-feet thick on the second floor. But the friars thought that the house had been hit by an earthquake.

The superior, two doors down from Padre Pio's room, heard the crash and rushed into Padre Pio's room. He found him on the floor, bleeding from his forehead, but with a pillow under his head.

"Padre," he cried, "what happened? How did you get there? Who put the pillow under your head?"

"The Madonna," Padre Pio answered.

The following morning, another priest continued the exorcism of the woman. As he began, the devil again shrieked out through the woman: "Last night I was up to see the old man upstairs. I hate him so much because he is a fountain of Faith. I would have done more, except the Lady in white stopped me."

"We believed what Padre Pio told us," said a Brother who was an eyewitness. "But the day after he was attacked we were able to connect the two statements: Padre Pio's assertion that the Madonna had put the pillow under his head, and the devil's boast that he would have done more if the Lady had not stopped him."

This same Brother described how Padre Pio looked. "His face was cut above the right eyebrow. His eyes were black, all black under his eyes. It looked like he took charcoal and underlined his eyes. His shoulders were terribly bruised. I saw it."

For five days, Padre Pio's face was so disfigured that he dared not say Mass in public. Some oversolicitous women of the town, ignorant of what had happened, criticized the Capuchins for restricting Padre Pio.

Two years later, a woman said to him: "Padre, the last time I was here was when the little devil hurt you."

"Little devil!" Padre Pio retorted. "They weren't little at all. They had the hooves of Lucifer to beat me with."

Padre Raffaele, for thirty years Padre Pio's confrere, told me that Padre Pio one morning had sharp pains in his arms and legs. Padre Pio said that it was rheumatism. "We called in a well-known doctor," Padre Raffaele said, "and the doctor said it was not rheumatism, but that Padre Pio's bones were broken. We called in Maestro Vincenzo, who set the broken bones."

Even if Padre Pio were some kind of a psychopath, he could not have inflicted that kind of punishment on himself.

It is amazing that the devil's assaults did not make

Padre Pio psychotic. Even more amazing was Padre Pio's ability to show a sense of humor when the devil assailed him. We already referred to the game he played with Barbablu. Without intruding into the field of medicine and psychiatry, we can see in Padre Pio's sense of humor a proof of his sanity and emotional equilibrium.

A priest who lived with Padre Pio told me the story he had heard from a lady who moved to San Giovanni Rotondo. When she arrived, she was lonely and depressed. For six weeks her arm was badly swollen. Padre Pio appeared to her in a dream. He pressed both thumbs on her arm, and in the morning the arm was completely cured. She then could make her own bed, lift a chair, and do things which she had not been able to do for many weeks.

Some months afterwards, she asked Padre Pio if he were the one who had appeared to her and cured her. Padre Pio said: "*Si*, yes." Years later, conditions in her native Austria made her very sad, and she began to cry. Again Padre Pio appeared to her at her bedside, with a large cross which she recognized as the cross in the friars' chapel. Padre Pio blessed her with it, and she immediately felt consoled and at peace.

On her nameday, July 26, the Feast of St. Anne, she asked Padre Pio whether it was he who had appeared to her and had blessed her. Again he said: "*Si*." She then asked why he had blessed her.

"To drive away the evil spirits," he answered.

She understood Padre Pio to say that she had been possessed. She was terrified. But she could not ask him for an explanation because she did not speak Italian very well. But Padre Pio answered her unspoken question: "I did not drive the devil *out of* you, but *away from* you."

Accounts of assaults by the devil read like weird medieval legends. But the life of Padre Pio is not a medieval legend. It is as contemporary as Rod Serling's *Night Gallery*. Only the characters were not phantom images on a television tube. They were as real as the girl who one day sauntered down the aisle of the crowded church of San Giovanni Rotondo. "You sinners!" she shouted, "you are very bad people. You are ungrateful!" Her face was contorted, her eyes flashed. The people fled in terror.

Up and down the aisle she strutted. "I'm the owner of this church, and I'm the only person who gives orders here." Obviously referring to Padre Pio, the devil within her continued to shout: "You see someone else's footprints here, but I'm the owner."

Then, walking over to the picture of St. Michael, she boasted against the Archangel who hurled Lucifer from Heaven: "You didn't win! I won!"

Padre Pio was in the sacristy at the time, hearing the confession of a man. He interrupted the confession and made a move toward the door of the church. "The girl is possessed," the sacristan warned. "Don't go out."

"Don't be afraid," the Padre answered him calmly. "When were we afraid of the devil?"

As he approached the girl, she crouched near his confessional and waited for him like a tigress ready to spring.

"Go away from there," he said firmly.

"Please don't send me away, please don't, please don't," she pleaded, already yielding to the stronger hand of the priest. "Please don't send me away!"

"Go away until I finish hearing confessions," he demanded. "Then come back here." She obeyed.

When she returned, he ordered her: "Go into the confessional." Again she obeyed. Padre Pio waited a few minutes, and then listened to her very long confession. "She left the confessional," an observer mentioned, "with her face transformed like that of an Angel."

Not all, but most instances of diabolical possession involved women. One case was that of a young married woman. She was carried on a stretcher from the Casa Sollievo, Padre Pio's hospital, to the church. For over a year she had never awakened from a deep sleep. When Padre Pio gave the blessing at Benediction of the Blessed Sacrament, she awoke, snorted like a bull, and her body began to puff up. Her hair was disheveled, her dress in disarray.

Taking the woman and her husband into the sacristy, Padre Pio began the prayer of exorcism. As he prayed, the woman tried frantically to claw his habit and his beard. Without flinching, Padre Pio finished the prayer and walked away. Peace was restored. The young wife gently grasped her husband's arm and left the sacristy with him. She sat down quietly in church and asked her husband for a comb.

In 1952, the case involving Maria Carboni caused quite a sensation. For six weeks she had suffered periods of delirium, especially at night. Doctors diagnosed her illness in various ways, some as cerebral congestion, some as hysteria.

It soon became apparent that some evil mysterious force was at work. During the day she was normal. At night she became violent. She beat herself and talked with the devil. She knew to the minute how long these conversations would last.

No one but the child saw the devil, but everyone sensed his presence. Maria described him as red and black. During his attacks the windows rattled. Loud knocking was heard on the door.

Word about Maria spread, and morbid curiosity seekers flocked to see her suffer and scream and recite poems in classical languages completely unknown to her.

Don Deglesositi, her pastor, at first dismissed the reports about Maria as hysteria. He soon changed his mind.

"For three nights," he said, "the girl had such severe attacks that four persons could hardly keep her in bed. Her eyes were closed. She screamed. Ten of us who were in her room heard the windows rattle, doors slam, and felt the whole house tremble."

One night during an attack, Maria announced that only Padre Pio could help her. Don Deglespositi hired a taxi, and with another priest, her brother, and another religious, set out for San Giovanni Rotondo.

On the way, the taxi had two flat tires, and the gas tank was damaged. Twice they collided with a truck, and Maria had thirty-three seizures before they reached their destination.

When they finally arrived in San Giovanni Rotondo, Maria was placed on a bench in the church to rest.

"Poor little thing (*poverina*)," Padre Pio said. "Who knows how much she has suffered? Let us hope she will become better."

He blessed her, and she was freed. It was the Feast of the Sacred Heart.

If dabblers in the occult could witness a case of possession and exorcism, they might be in less of a hurry to substitute the security of God for the fun and games of ouija boards, seances, card reading, trying to talk to the dead, and dealing with high priests of Satan and with Satan himself.

A resident of San Giovanni Rotondo told me of an incident which he witnessed on a hot summer evening. He was walking over to an ice cream concession, thoughts of the devil farthest from his mind. At the entrance to the church he saw a woman being held down in a chair by two stout men. She was hooting and howling like an animal. Her hair and scarf were messed, her dress was ripped, her shoes were off. Suddenly she sprang up from the chair, throwing the men backward. They grabbed her again and forced her back into the chair, but again she tossed them aside almost effortlessly. "She had the power of a horse," my friend told me.

Padre Pio was summoned. The moment he stood in front of her, she collapsed into the chair as if she were dead. There was not a movement, there was not a sound. Padre Pio blessed her and walked away.

"Then it started again," the man recalled. "I was scared, really scared. You could see something that was not human. I had never seen anything like it in my life. She started again to scream and howl and thrash around with superhuman force."

Possibly my friend knew the sequel to this episode, but his description stopped there. He would say no more, because that was all he had witnessed. Sometimes, as we know from Sacred Scripture, more than one devil has to be cast out. Sometimes an exorcism must be continued in stages even for one devil. In any case, the only events which he would describe were those which he had seen with his own eyes.

Another case which he observed involved a woman who had been brought into the church and seated in a pew to wait for Padre Pio's blessing. Suddenly, without a sound, she began slithering along the pews, twisting and writhing without letup like a snake in agony. "She could not have been putting on an act," he said. "Her movement was too unnatural, and it lasted too long."

Padre Carmelo, the superior, asked everyone to leave. He watched her carefully for awhile and then called Padre Pio. He blessed the woman and restored her to peace and to God.

In Milan, a certain boy grew up normally until he was six years old. Then he stopped speaking. Nobody could get a word out of him. His mother, a widow, took him from specialist to specialist, spending all the money she had on him. No one could help her or explain why her son could not talk. Medically he was perfect.

Six more years passed. When he was twelve, his mother brought him to Padre Pio and explained the whole story to him. "This is not a thing for medicine," the Padre answered. He made the Sign of the Cross over him and immediately the boy began to speak. This was witnessed by a group of friars and laymen.

The devil's attacks continued almost until the end of Padre Pio's life. When he was an eighty-year-old man, he was so feeble that he could not even turn over by himself in bed. He had to be lifted in and out of his arm chair. But sometimes he would be seated in his chair, praying the rosary as he always did, when suddenly he would be bounced out of his chair onto the floor.

"One morning," a confrere recalls, "Padre Onorato and I went downstairs for a cup of coffee. We had left Padre Pio with a buzzer attached to the arm of his chair. All he needed was a hand motion to call for help. Everything was fine. Within the space of five minutes, Padre Onorato returned and heard Padre Pio pleading out loud: 'Help me! Help me!' He rushed into the room and found Padre Pio sprawled on the floor, beaten and bruised."

Often Padre Pio sat on the veranda near his room, again, always praying the rosary. As he sat there, the devil would stalk around him. The Capuchins, who kept a constant vigil with him towards the end of his life, saw him looking around the bottom of his chair, back and forth, back and forth, watching something, staring at something real which nobody else could see.

"This made me feel eerie," a Brother said, "because we knew he saw something. This didn't happen only once, when he might have been looking at a piece of dust rolling around the floor. It happened almost every day."

Once Padre Mariano asked him: "What do you see?" He answered simply: "I see a head." Padre Mariano knew enough and respected him enough not to question him further.

His confreres never saw or felt anything. They seldom questioned him about the devil. One of them observed: "I think the devil was his constant companion. Padre Pio was very alert to unexpected movements and sounds. He said that the devil appeared to him in all shapes. He had fear even of a mouse, because the devil would start out as a mouse and turn into a claw and go for his eyes. It was fantastic!"

One day while Padre Raffaele was visiting him, Padre Pio suddenly snapped at him: "Turn around!" Padre Pio saw the devil go for Padre Raffaele and thought the devil was clutching at the back of his habit.

A two-way speaker was set up between Padre Pio's and Padre Alessio's rooms. It was always turned on. "In my room, which was very close to his," Padre Alessio recalls, "I could hear everything, even his breathing. I could hear every word. He was never unattended. I looked after him day and night. But I had to try to get some sleep to be able to help him during the day. One night he called me time after time. He called me every five or ten minutes. I got a bit upset."

"Why do you keep asking me to come?" Padre Alessio complained. "Then when I come, you don't have anything to say." All Padre Alessio could see was Padre Pio lying in bed, praying the rosary.

"My son," Padre Pio pleaded, "stay in this chair and sleep here. Stay here because they don't leave me alone. They don't give me even a minute's sleep."

Reflecting on these incidents, Padre Alessio said: "My presence would save him from something or from somebody. I don't know from whom, but I'm sure they were not Angels. This happened when he was seventy-eight years old, only three years before he died."

His battles with the devil were not the only afflictions he had to endure. His bronchial ailments continued to plague him. And worse, his eyesight went bad on him. "I cannot write to you (more often)," he wrote to Padre Benedetto, "because of my blessed eyesight."

It seems that at times he was completely blind. "My eyesight," he wrote to Padre Agostino on January 30, 1915, "has come back to me." He had a pair of eyeglasses, but for some unknown reason, he never wore them.

His trouble with his eyes was a serious and chronic condition. In 1916, twelve years after he first mentioned his poor eyesight, he wrote to Padre Benedetto:

"Father, I will now stop, because I am extremely tired especially with my poor eyesight. I feel very bad that you had to complain about my last report to you. But, my Father, there is a reason for this. I wrote the reason at the beginning of this letter. Another reason is the seriousness of my physical condition especially my eyesight. For three days I have been forcing myself to write this letter and I don't know how many more days it will take to finish. I have a splitting headache, and I can't concentrate. Sometimes this happens when the day is hot. It seems that I am losing my mind. With all these things you can understand how painful it is to write to you. I am very sorry to hear that you are not in good health, but I pray to God for you. Since I can't do anything else, I offer myself to God as a victim for you. Now that you are sick, I renew this offering to Jesus often."

His superiors were considerate. They willingly allowed him to spend most of his seminary years with his parents in Pietrelcina where the air is clean and crisp and the cool breeze is bracing. In 1912, they extended to him the privilege commonly accorded to blind priests, that of substituting the Mass of the Blessed Mother or the Mass for the Dead in place of the prescribed formulas.

He was also exempted from the obligation of reading the Divine Office each day, the ancient, official prayer of the Church which all priests are expected to say daily. He was allowed to substitute the recitation of the rosary.

Besides his ill health, there was another problem he had to deal with. In Italy, there was universal military conscription. Priests and seminarians were not exempt, although they were usually given noncombatant positions.

Padre Pio's call came on November 6, 1915. He was assigned to the medical corps in Naples. But within six weeks he was given a one-year leave of absence because of his poor health, and he returned to Pietrelcina.

During that year, he paid a few visits to the ancient Friary of Our Lady of Grace, at San Giovanni Rotondo. Connected with the friary was a minor seminary, where boys studied who were thinking of joining the Capuchin Order. Later on, he would be permanently assigned there.

When his leave of absence was up, he returned to Naples. Twelve days later he was given his second medical leave, this time for six months. He divided his time between Pietrelcina and San Giovanni Rotondo.

After the six months expired and Padre Pio had not returned to Naples, the Army considered him a deserter and sent two Military Police to Pietrelcina to arrest him. They searched all over for Francesco Forgione, but nobody admitted even knowing him. Possibly the people were being coy in covering up for him, or possibly they thought of him only as Padre Pio.

Finally the M.P.'s located Padre Pio's sister. She told the officers that he was known as Padre Pio and could be found at San Giovanni Rotondo. The officers went to San Giovanni Rotondo, arrested him and brought him back to Naples. He was saved from prosecution, however, when he produced his papers which allowed him "to go home for six months and await instructions." "My instructions," he said, "didn't come until today."

After another leave of absence because of double bronchitis, he was finally declared medically unfit for military service. He was offered a pension but refused it. He said he had done nothing to deserve it. "If I had kept my pension for these fifty years," he joked when he was in his seventies, "I'd be the richest man in the world."

The Provincial Superior wanted to station Padre Pio at San Giovanni Rotondo but thought that his tubercular condition would be a danger to the boys. However, Padre Pio assured him that his illness "was not for others."

The Provincial yielded and appointed him as spiritual director of the boys in the seminary.

Padre Pio took up residence in San Giovanni Rotondo on May 13, 1918. He remained there until his death in 1968. These dates are highly significant, not merely because they chronicle events in his life, but because from May 13, 1918, onward, he never left the town of San Giovanni Rotondo. Nevertheless, there is no doubt that he has been seen in many cities around the world. If there is any validity to rules for judging authenticity of documents and the truth of witnesses, these facts force us to conclude that Padre Pio had the gift of bilocation, the ability to be in two places at one time.

We would be getting ahead of our story if we should discuss his bilocation at this point. We will add a chapter on it later. For the present, let us simply continue to unroll the ribbon of events as they happened.

As we said, Padre Pio took up permanent residence in San Giovanni Rotondo in 1918. It is a sun-baked town tucked away in the mountains of the Gargano Peninsula, which commands a breathtaking view of the Gulf of Manfredonia and the Adriatic Sea. The town seems to be pasted right into the middle of the 3,275-foot Gargano Mountains, on which evergreens and a few shade trees struggle for a grip among the rocks. When Padre Pio first arrived there, there were fewer than 3,000 people. Today, it is a city of about 20,000. It is about fourteen miles from Foggia and twenty-five miles from Manfredonia.

The name of the town might be translated "St. John in the Round." Its Patron Saint is St. John the Baptist, or *San Giovanni* in Italian. The "Rotondo" is a flashback to the days of the ancient Roman Empire, when a temple was built there to the pagan god Janus. The temple was in-the-round to accommodate the god who had two faces, one supposedly looking to the past and the other to the future.

The church and friary there were built in 1616 and

dedicated to Our Lady of Grace, *Santa Maria delle Grazie*. When the convento, the residence of the Capuchins, was rebuilt in 1692, it had only three rooms. The same old friary still stands, although it was added to three times. It now has living quarters for about twenty priests and Brothers.

In 1959, a new church was built wall-to-wall with the old but smaller church. Services are still conducted in both churches.

CHAPTER 4

Prelude to the Stigmata

Strangely, few authors mention anything about the stigmata which Padre Pio received visibly before 1918. With dutiful reliance one upon the other, they mention that he received "the invisible stigmata" in 1915 and "the visible stigmata" in 1918.

However, we have a first-hand account of Padre Pio himself, which attests that he first received the stigmata visibly in 1910. We can establish that year from a letter dated September 8, 1911, which he wrote to Padre Benedetto:

"Yesterday evening something happened which I am unable to explain or understand. In the center of the palms of my hands a redness appeared about the size of a centesimo (penny). In the center of that red spot there was also an intense and acute pain. This pain was worse in the middle of my left hand, so much so that the pain still persists. Even under my feet I can feel some pain. *This phenomenon has taken place on and off for almost a year* (italics added), although lately it has been some time since it occurred. It doesn't get any better, however, and now for the first time I shall tell you about it. The reason is that I have always been overcome by that evil called shame. If you only knew, even now, how I have had to fight with myself to tell you about it! There are many things I want to tell you, but words fail me. I will tell you this much, however, that my heart beats violently when I find myself before Jesus in the Holy Eucharist. Sometimes it feels as if my heart wants to jump out of my chest. At times, while at the altar I feel my whole being burning up in a way that I cannot describe. It seems to me that especially my face is about to go up in flames. My Father, I do not know what these signs mean."

In this letter Padre Pio speaks only of a "redness" in the center of his hands. However, in his letter of October 10, 1915, he at least implies that he had actual wounds (*trafitture*, literally "transfixions,") which he contrasts to keen pains (*dolore*).

These wounds disappeared after a few days, but the incident was repeated almost every week until 1918. He speaks of the visible wounds only in his hands. If they appeared also in his feet and side, we do not know. He does speak of the *pain* in his feet.

Six months later he describes another traumatic experience, which authors commonly call the "transfixion" of his heart. Again, he makes no mention of any external wound in his side, but only the agony in his heart. On March 21, 1912, he wrote to Padre Agostino:

"From Thursday evening until Saturday, and also on Tuesday, I experience excruciating agony. My heart, my hands and my feet seem transfixed with a sword. I feel tremendous pain. The devil never stops appearing in horrible shapes and punching me in a frightful way. But long live Jesus who consoles me with His visits. This same Jesus keeps asking me for more and more of my love, and my heart rather than my mouth responds: 'I need to love you more and more, but I don't have any more love in my heart. I have given all my love to you. If you want more, fill my heart with your love, and then oblige me to love you more and I will not refuse you.' "

Again, in 1912, on August 26, Padre Pio wrote to Padre Agostino:

"Listen to what happened to me last Friday (August 23, 1912). I was in the church making my thanksgiving after Mass, when suddenly I felt my heart wounded by a fiery arrow which burned with such intensity that I thought I would certainly die. I cannot find the right words to make you understand the intensity of this flame. Do you believe me? My soul, the victim of this consolation, could only stand by in silence. I felt as though an invisible force had plunged me completely into the fire. My God, what a fire it was! What sweetness! I have experienced many of these transports of love. They were many, and they lasted a long time, but the fire was less intense. But this time, one more second and my soul would have been separated from my body. . . . I would have gone to Jesus. Oh what a beautiful thing to become a victim of love."

Few people realized the metamorphosis which God was rendering in the soul of the young priest. At that time, to his confreres, he was only a man who disturbed the peace of all by the noise in his room. To the laity, he was a "crazy monk" who detained them over two hours when celebrating Mass.

But Padre Agostino realized that something supernatural was happening. Again he pressed Padre Pio for details. He wrote to him on September 30, 1915:

"Now I ask you in the name of Jesus certain things which you must not forget to answer. You must pray. I want to insist that Jesus will let me know everything, first for His glory and then for the salvation of souls. Tell me:

"(1) When did Jesus begin to favor you with the heavenly visions?

"(2) Has He granted you the indescribable gift of

His stigmata even though it be invisible? Has He allowed you to experience His crowning with thorns and His scourging, and how many times?

"I am not merely curious, for Jesus sees my intention. You must pray and you must answer me although I am resigned to whatever Jesus wishes, but I beg a reply from you."

Padre Pio acknowledged his letter on October 10th, 1915:

"I cannot help but recognize the express will of God in your persistent desire to learn, or rather, to receive answers to your questions. And so with trembling hands and with a heart filled to the brim with pain, and not knowing the reason for this, I hasten to obey you. Your first question is: you wish to know when Jesus began to favor His poor creature with His heavenly appearances. If I am not mistaken, these began soon after my novitiate year. (His novitiate year extended from January 1903 to January 1904.)

"Your second question is: Has He granted the indescribable gift of His sacred stigmata. To this I must answer in the affirmative. The first time that Jesus deigned to grant this favor, they were visible, especially in one hand, and, since my soul was so terrified by such a visible phenomenon, I begged the Lord to take them away. And so they disappeared. However, although the open wounds disappeared, the keen pain accompanying them didn't go away, and this I specifically experienced in certain circumstances and on definite days.

"Your third and last question is: Whether the Lord has permitted me to experience, and how many times, His crown of thorns and His scourging. The answer to this question must also be in the affirmative. I can only say that this soul has suffered like this for a few years,

and about once a week. I think I have obeyed you, haven't
I?''

For eight years the hammer of God pounded out
these stigmata on the anvil of Padre Pio's body. Another
blow had yet to crash down to forge on his body the image
of Jesus Christ crucified.

It came on August 5, 1918. Writers refer to this traumatic encounter with Christ as "the transverberation of
the heart." It is tremendously important in Padre Pio's
life. Yet authors of books in English seem to be completely ignorant of it. Padre Pio wrote to Padre Benedetto on October 22, 1918:

"I cannot tell you what happened in that moment,
which was a moment of sheer martyrdom. On the evening of the 5th, I was hearing a boy's confession (a semi-
narian at San Giovanni Rotondo) when all of a sudden I
saw a most exalted heavenly person (*personaggio*). I
was plunged into extreme terror. He stood before the eye
of my mind, holding some kind of special instrument in
his hand, like a very long iron spear with a well-sharp-
ened point. It seemed that fire shot out from this point.

"Seeing this person and watching him plunge the instrument violently into my soul happened in an instant. I
groaned with pain and felt as if I were dying. I told the
boy to go away because I felt ill and didn't have the
strength to continue.

"This agony lasted without interruption until the
morning of August 7. I can't tell you what I suffered during this period of torment. It seemed that even my vis-
cera were being pulled out by that spear. Every fiber of
my being was consumed by fire. From that day on, I have
been wounded almost to the point of death. In the inmost
part of my soul I feel a wound that is always open, which
makes me suffer constant pain."

The symphony is continuing. For thirty years its
theme, Padre Pio's love for God and God's love for him,
has been ringing loud and clear through the harmony and

cacophony of his life. Now a crescendo will climax on September 20, 1918 and will continue to echo for fifty years, from the Gargano Mountains to Europe, the Americas, and to the Far East.

CHAPTER 5

The Stigmata

The most spectacular event of Padre Pio's life was the permanent reception of the stigmata, the wounds of the crucifixion in his hands, his feet and side. Myriad books and articles have been written about Padre Pio's stigmata, some of them accurate, some of them absurd.

"Padre Pio doesn't need any exaggeration," said Fr. Dominic Meyer, the Milwaukee-born Capuchin secretary of Padre Pio for seven years. "The truth about him," he said, "is fantastic enough."

The truth, the truth, the truth! Stick to the truth! That is what I heard from the intimates of Padre Pio when engaged in my research on him.

Even when I asked innocuous questions about the Casa Sollievo, Padre Pio's hospital, I received guarded answers. "We want you to write just what is true," Miss Lucibelli, a spokesman for the Casa, admonished. "We have to be very prudent about these things, to say just what is true, no more, and no less."

An abundance of objective source material is available for the asking. This heightens the mystery why journalists do not use the primary source of information,

Padre Pio's own description of what happened. Perhaps we can best learn what happened if we string together four letters, one of them written two weeks before September 20, and three of them written after the 20th.

The first letter which we quote was written by Padre Pio. It is dated September 5, 1918:

"I see myself submerged in an ocean of fire. Blood, blood continues without ceasing to pour out of the wound which has been opened again. This alone is enough to make me die a thousand times over. Oh my God, why do I not die? Or do you not see that the very life of the soul you wounded is in torment? Are you so cruel that you remain deaf to my cries of pain? I am not asking for comfort. What can I say? Forgive me, Father, I am beside myself, and I don't know what I am saying. The intense pain of the open wound makes me angry against my will. It leads me to the point of delirium."

The second letter which we quote was written by Padre Pio on October 17, 1918. Although he does not directly talk about the stigmata, this is his first letter after receiving the stigmata, and it shows the helplessness of the poor Capuchin friar pursued without respite by the Hound of Heaven:

"I have endured terrible and sorrowful hours. I die every moment, physically and morally. My soul doesn't know God. Oh God of my soul, where are you? Where have you gone to hide? Where can I meet you again? Where can I look for you? Don't you see, oh Jesus, that my soul really and truly would like to listen to you? It is searching for you everywhere, but you do not let it find you except in the height of your wrath and filled to the brim with trouble and bitterness.

"What can possibly express how serious my situation is? I cannot tell you in human language all that I want in the reflection of your light. When I try to tell you something by babbling, my soul discovers that it was wrong again and had not strayed at all from the truth.

"You are all that I have. Have you given me up for ever? I want to shout and cry as loud as I possibly can, but I am completely feeble, and no strength remains within me to match my will. What shall I do but let this cry rise to your throne: My God, my God, why have you forsaken me?

"My soul is laid out as a picture of my misery. My God! Grant that I may bear up under this pitiful sight. Shield me by reflecting this ray of light away from me, because I cannot endure such stark contrast. My Father, in your splendor I can see in full all my wickedness and my ingratitude. My God! Join me right now with your help, because left to myself, I tremble, faithless, an ungrateful creature before his Creator who can protect him from his powerful enemies.

"I did not appreciate your choicest favors, and now I see myself sentenced to live alone with my shortcomings, stooped over, veering from a straight line in all that I do. Your hand keeps bearing down more heavily upon me. Alas! Who will deliver me from myself? Who will rescue me from the body of this death? Who will extend a hand to keep me from being swept up and swallowed by a vast and deep ocean? Is it necessary that I resign myself to be engulfed by this storm which always keeps growing more and more fierce? Is it necessary that I utter that 'be it done to me' as I stare at that mysterious Person who has stigmatized my whole body and does not desist from His painful, bitter, cutting and penetrating work? Before the old wounds have had a chance to heal, He doesn't give me a moment's rest before He comes to reopen the same wounds in an infinite crucible within this victim.

"Please, my Father, come to help me, please! Everything inside of me is raining blood, and sometimes even my bodily eyes are forced to submit to look on the bloody torrent of this stream. Please! Stop this torture for me, this condemnation, this humiliation, this confusion! My soul can no longer endure it, nor does it know how to put up with it. How many things there are, my Father, that I want to say, but the suffocating overflow of my suffering leaves me mute. Give me the kindness of hearing from you with your usual prompt charity, and be sure I will thank you and pray always for you.

> "Bless me always,
> "Fra Pio, Capuchin"

These two letters were like a sputtering fuse in comparison to his letter of October 22. That letter was like a bomb which was to explode five days later. But before we quote that letter, by far the most important of the entire *Epistolario*, we ought to inject a letter here written by Padre Benedetto, Padre Pio's spiritual director.

Padre Benedetto already knew of the appearance and disappearance of the wounds over the past decade. He had learned that something apparently more spectacular had happened to Padre Pio, and he wanted to find out what it was. He wrote to Padre Pio on October 19, 1918:

"My son, tell me everything, and tell it to me clearly. Do not only hint. What was it that that person did? Where does the blood flow from, and how many times a day or week? What is it that appears on your hands and feet, and how? I want to know *every single little detail* and under holy obedience. . . .

"Answer me, and tell me everything. Out of charity and obedience, do not conceal any of these things from me."

Padre Pio's reply to his spiritual director is, I feel, the most sublime treasure in the *Epistolario*. Because of its exceptional importance, I will translate it in its entirety, prefacing it with a few explanatory remarks:

1. The time of the event described in the letter was between 11:00 o'clock in the morning and 12:00 noon.

2. After celebrating Mass, Padre Pio, who was the

director of the seminary, accompanied the boys to the dining room for their breakfast. He himself never ate breakfast. When they had finished their meal, he returned to the choir in the upper rear section of the Church of Our Lady of Grace, where the choir loft is traditionally situated in a church. In this choir, the Capuchin community gathered for their daily community prayers and the chanting of the Divine Office.

3. Padre Pio either knelt or sat on one of the wooden benches, in front of a wooden crucifix which is three feet high and one inch thick. The figure of Jesus on this cross is not the clean, polished white corpus to which we are accustomed. The ribs and muscles of Jesus bulge out in high relief. The face is contorted in agony. Real and long iron spikes, capped with large heads, affix the hands to the beam. The arms and legs are disjointed.

4. The suffix *"aggio"* which Padre Pio uses to describe the person (*personaggio*) whom he saw, denotes grandeur and majesty. It is opposed to *"etto,"* a diminutive which connotes familiarity and affection.

5. It seems obvious that the *"personaggio"* whom he saw was Our Lord Himself. All that went before, and all that happened afterwards, blend perfectly into a beautiful unity. We have every reason to believe that the person who stamped the body of Padre Pio was the same Jesus Christ who marked the body of St. Francis of Assisi with the same seal of approval seven hundred years previously.

6. The letter is No. 510 in the *Epistolario*, pages 1,092 to 1,095.

7. The "J-M-J-D-F-C" at the beginning of the letter are the abbreviations of Jesus, Mary, Joseph, Dominic, Francis and Catherine of Siena, to whom he had special devotion.

This is the letter to Padre Benedetto:

"San Giovanni Rotondo
"22 October, 1918
"J.M.J.D.F.C.

"My most dear Father, may Jesus, the Sun
of Justice always shine on your spirit, mysteriously shrouded in obscurity in this ordeal which
has been willed directly by Jesus Himself!

"Oh Father, why are you so upset, so fearful? Be calm, because Jesus is with you and is
pleased with you. My soul is torn, experiencing
such great spiritual suffering. Oh, how I have
prayed and prayed for you to Our Lord, who lets
me feel in my heart that He is with you always,
that He has doubled for you His graces, His concern, His abundant Love.

"How can you think that God has allowed
calamities to rage around you and that you have
caused all of this? Oh Father, do not be afraid,
for goodness sake. You are not at fault in the
roaring of this storm. You shouldn't have any
fear for your soul. Jesus is with you, and you are
very dear to Him. All this is the truth before
God. Be at peace, and let the Lord give you the
trials He wants. This will all redound to your
sanctification. I didn't keep silent in my last letter, not at all, out of false piety, as you scolded
me for not having agreed with all that has built
up within you because of the impenitence of
your soul. Your fear was groundless. I kept silent because I did not feel the strength to repri-
mand you. Please, for goodness sake, don't attribute this fault to the goodness of God, who
doesn't want to have anything come from a mis-
understanding.

"God can use a scourge for His purpose in
leading men to approach the Divinity as their
principal end. God's secondary and immediate

purpose is to keep men from persecuting the sons of God who are on the side of the real winners of the present battle. Don't be so afraid, because iniquity will not go so far as to overwhelm righteousness, but the iniquities themselves will be overwhelmed and justice will triumph.

"What can I tell you about that which you asked me with regard to my crucifixion. My God, the confusion and humiliation which I feel in manifesting that which you have wrought in this mean creature!

"It was the morning of the 20th of last month. I was in the choir after the celebration of holy Mass, when I was overcome with drowsiness as of a sweet sleep. All my internal and external senses, and also the faculties of my soul, experienced an indescribable quiet. During all of this, there was total silence, within me and around me. Then, suddenly, a grand sense of peace and abandonment came over me, to the complete exclusion of everything else. I remained in that state, crushed. This all happened in a flash.

"While this was happening, I discovered myself in front of a mysterious, exalted person (*personaggio*), similar to the person whom I saw on the evening of the 5th of August. The only difference was that this person was spilling out blood from his hands and feet and heart.

"I was terrified when I saw him. What I felt at that time, I cannot explain. I felt as if I were going to die, and I would have died if my Lord had not intervened and sustained my heart, which I felt was pounding its way right out of my chest.

"The vision of the person faded away, and I

noticed that my hands and feet and chest had been pierced and were bleeding profusely. Imagine the confusion which I experienced then and which I experience continuously almost every day.

"The wound of the heart pours out blood profusely, especially from Thursday evening until Saturday. My Father, I am dying from suffering, through the pain and the confusion which I feel in my inmost soul. I fear that I will die from the loss of blood if my Lord does not heed the groans of my poor health and stop what is happening.

"Will He take away this confusion which I am experiencing from this external sign? I will cry to Him at the top of my voice and will not stop begging Him, so that in His mercy He will take away not the suffering, not the pain, because it is impossible, and I want to be inebriated with pain. But I will beg Him to remove these external signs which utterly confuse me and cause indescribable and unbearable humiliation. The person of whom I intended to speak in my previous letter is none other than the one of whom I spoke in my last letter, the person whom I saw on the 5th of August. He pursues his work relentlessly, with extreme torture of the soul. I feel a constant roaring within myself, as that of a waterfall, always cascading blood. My God! Your chastisement is just and your judgment is right. Use me to show your mercy. Oh Lord, I will always say with your prophet, do not censure in your anger nor chastise me in your wrath. My Father, now that all of my inmost being is known to you, do not disdain to speak a word of comfort in the midst of this sea of cruel and harsh bitterness.

"I pray always for you, for my poor Padre Agostino, and for everyone.

"Bless me always.

"Your most affectionate son,
"Fra Pio"

Padre Pio's awesome description of that event is only one stroke on the picture which we have of his conformity to Jesus Christ. He continued to describe what was happening, now in a letter to Padre Benedetto, dated December 20, 1918:

"For many days I have been aware of something like a shaft of iron entering from the bottom of my heart and penetrating through to the lower part of my right shoulder. It causes me excruciating pain and does not let me get a bit of sleep. Now what is happening to me?"

What *was* happening? God the Father was putting the finishing touches on this Capuchin carbon copy of Jesus Christ. Externally, he even looked like Jesus crucified. In his mind and soul, he thought like Jesus.

"I offered myself to God as a victim for you," he wrote to Padre Benedetto. A simple statement, but as profound as Sacred Scripture. Padre Pio apparently found it within himself to ignore his stigmata, his blindness, his temptations, and beatings by the devil, a splitting headache and a brutally hot summer day. "I'm very sorry," he wrote, "to hear that you are not in good health. But I pray to God for you. Since I cannot do anything else, I offered myself to God as a victim for you."

CHAPTER 6

Eyewitness Reports

Padre Pio's sufferings were only one jaw of the vise which squeezed him. On the other side were the doctors. "Better a mouse between two cats," he joked, "than Padre Pio between two doctors." But when Padre Pio saw that some doctors took him too literally, he quipped: "At least the mouse can run away."

Of course, his stigmata could not go undetected. His confreres saw him limping, his sleeves pulled down over his hands. Padre Paolino, his local superior, insisted that Padre Pio tell him what had happened. He was the first person to hear that amazing account of the 20th. He notified his Provincial Superior of what he had heard.

Padre Pio's wounds were first photographed by Padre Placido, another Capuchin priest living with him. On September 30, he told Padre Pio that he had Padre Paolino's permission to take his picture and invited Padre Pio to step into the garden. He had a pre-focused camera in his sleeve and asked Padre Pio to cross his arms. Before Padre Pio realized what was happening, Padre Placido whipped out his camera and snapped a picture. Padre Pio took it all in fun, one time looking down piously, another time holding a lamb, just as Padre Placido asked him.

Padre Paolino did not have to command Padre Pio to pose for the pictures, as some romantic writers would have us believe. Nor did his confreres begin to treat him as a mini-god. Life in a Capuchin friary goes on normally, even if a man is a stigmatic.

The Father Provincial was not quite so casual. He commissioned Dr. Luigi Romanelli, the Chief of Staff of the City Hospital of Barletta, to examine Padre Pio. Before this examination, Padre Pio tried desperately to stop the bleeding and to heal the wounds. Twice a week for several months he applied iodine to them. It did neither good nor harm.

Dr. Romanelli conducted five examinations over a period of fifteen months. In November, 1920, he submitted this report:

"Padre Pio has a very deep cut in the fifth intercostal space on the left side, 7 or 8 cms. long (about 2-3/4 or 3 inches), parallel to the ribs. The depth is great, but it is very difficult to ascertain. On his hand, there is an abundance of arterial blood. The borders of the wounds are not inflamed. They are very sensitive to the least pressure. The lesions in his hands are covered with a dark red membrane, but there is neither any edema (swelling) or any inflammation. When I pressed with my fingers on the palm and back of his hand there was a sensation of an empty space. By pressing like that you cannot tell whether the wounds (on the front and back of the hands) are joined together, because the strong pressure causes the subject intense pain. However, I repeated the painful experiment several times, in the morning and in the evening, and I must admit that each time I came to the same conclusion.

"The lesions of the feet have the same characteristics as those of the hands, but because of the thickness of the foot, it was difficult to experiment as accurately on the feet as on the hands.

"I have examined Padre Pio five times in the course of fifteen months, and while I have sometimes noted some modifications in the lesions, I have never been able to classify them in any known clinical order."

On July 26, 1919, one month after Dr. Romanelli began his investigations, another doctor was commissioned, this time by the Vatican. He was Dr. Amico Bignami, Professor of Pathology at the Royal University in Rome. He prided himself as an atheist and a positivist. That is, his starting point was the denial of anything which could not be proved scientifically. Dr. Bignami visited Padre Pio only once, and then issued this strange report:

"The physiological state of the sick man is normal. The wounds in the thorax (chest), the hands and feet, could have had their beginning by a multiple neurotic necrosis of the skin (i.e., death of living tissues caused by his nervousness). Their symmetry could have been completed by an unconscious phenomenon of auto-suggestion and could have been maintained artificially by the acid of tincture of iodine, which the sick man administered to himself, even though some doctors deny that that could cause the caustic and irritating burning."

Dr. Bignami considered his job completed. There was no need to investigate further. He applied ointment to Padre Pio's hands, bandaged them, and told him to leave them that way for a few days. The wounds, he thought, would go away. To Dr. Bignami, the case of Padre Pio was closed.

The General Superiors of the Capuchin Order in Rome were dissatisfied with Dr. Bignami's report. They commissioned another doctor who was also a surgeon, Giorgio Festa, to examine Padre Pio on October 9, 1919. His medical practice in Rome led many people to consider him one of the city's finest doctors. Among his other duties he was the head doctor and surgeon for the Capuchins at their Motherhouse in Rome.

Dr. Festa was amazed at the offhand manner of Dr. Bignami's report. He bristled at Dr. Bignami's statement that the irritation of the wounds in the soles of the feet could have come from repeated applications of tincture of iodine. Dr. Festa did not think that that was physically possible. Moreover, Padre Pio never used iodine after Dr. Bignami's examination.

After his examination he wrote: "In the palm of his left hand, more or less corresponding to the middle of the third metacarpal, I saw the existence of an anatomical lesion, round in shape, with clearly defined outer edges. In size it is a little more than 2 cm. (about 3/4 of an inch) in diameter."

The doctor then describes at some length how "the lesion is covered with a reddish brown scab which appears on any normal wound. On contact with the air, blood usually begins to coagulate and a healing process starts. But in the case of Padre Pio's wounds, the edges of the scab detach themselves and begin to flake towards the center of the wound. Eventually the whole scab falls off. The wound is continuously bloody and keeps forming this kind of a scab."

The doctor continues:

"The area of the lesion in the palm which I have just described has a clearly marked border, so that the surrounding skin, when I examined it with a powerful magnifying glass, showed no signs of edema, no sign of redness, no sign of infection, and not the tiniest indication of having been struck.

"The metacarpal bone shows no anatomical discontinuity, and although slightly enlarged in the middle section it appears to be regular in the rest of its length. On the reverse side of the same left hand, more clearly in line with the metacarpal bone of the third finger, and therefore not corresponding exactly with the palm side, there is also a lesion similar to the other one in shape and appearance, which seems to be more restricted and apparently with a more superficial scab. Lesions which exist on both sides of the right hand can be similarly described. During my examination, tiny and continuous drops of blood oozed out of the lesions.

"When I asked him to make a fist, he could not close his hand completely. It was only with very great difficulty that he could bend the tips of his fingers in toward the palm of his hand.

"During my visit, in order to observe the lesions on his feet more easily, I myself helped him to remove his socks. I clearly saw that they were stained with bloody serum. On the top part of both feet, precisely corresponding with the second metatarsus, I noticed circular lesions, reddish brown in color, covered with a soft scab and of the same character and origin as the lesion of the hand which I described. These wounds were perhaps a little smaller and more superficial than those of the hand. Even here, the entire length of the metatarsal bone was not broken. There was no trace of infection, no edema, no inflammatory reaction in the skin surrounding the lesions. There, too, was a slow but continuous oozing of the bloody serum.

"On the soles of the feet, at a point corresponding to the top of the feet, I observed two other lesions, one in the sole of each foot, with clearly defined edges, perfectly identical to the wounds on the top, and all bloody.

"When pressure was applied directly to each of these tissues, whether on the hand or on the foot, no matter how gently the pressure was applied, it always evoked a feeling of very intense pain. There was also a feeling of pain in the area surrounding the lesion, but the pain was less intense.

"If I were to be interrogated by superior authorities on this particular question, I would have to answer and confirm under oath, so much is the certitude of the impression received, that I would be able to read something or to see an object if it were placed behind the hand."

Mrs. William Sanguinetti, the wife of Padre Pio's former personal physician and still a resident in San Giovanni Rotondo, said that she remembered the days when Padre Pio offered Mass at St. Anthony's altar in the old church. There is a window behind the altar, and when Padre Pio raised his hands, she could see a shaft of light pass through them.

Instead of ending his diagnosis with one visit, as did Dr. Bignami, Dr. Festa resolved to perform another examination. He arranged a second visit, accompanied by Dr. Romanelli and the Provincial Superior, on July 15, 1918.

Dr. Festa removed Padre Pio's sandals, and the group immediately saw a large circular stain, moist and reddish on the bottom of both socks. The stains very clearly were blood and could have come only from some kind of a wound. It was apparent that the wounds were not the result of the continuous application of iodine but real, starkly real wounds.

Dr. Festa continued at considerable length to refute Dr. Bignami's hypothesis that the iodine was responsible in any way for the appearance of the wounds. The repeated applications of iodine, said Dr. Festa, certainly could not have caused a very sharp demarcation between the redness of the circular wound and the white skin around it.

"I have visual documentation," Dr. Festa wrote, "of the reality of these lesions. I have preserved two white woolen socks which Padre Pio had worn for a very short time. Each of these clearly showed a large bloodstain, round in shape, still reddish in color with bits of blood clots adhering to it. These stains correspond to the places where the four wounds appear, namely: one on top of the left foot, one on top of the right foot, one on bottom of the left foot, and one on bottom of the right foot."

About the wound in Padre Pio's side, Dr. Festa wrote:

"On the left side of the chest region of the body there is a final lesion in the form of an upside-down cross. The perpendicular part measures about 7 cm. (2-3/4 inches). The line begins at about the fifth rib and slants down toward the cartilage border of the ribs. The horizontal part of the cross is about 4 cm. (about 1-1/2 inches) long. It does not intersect at right angles but at a slant, a point 5 cm. (about 2 inches) down from the point where the perpendicular bar begins. It seems to spread out and become more straight as it reaches the lower extremity.

"This figure of a cross is merely on the surface. The two lines are about as thick as 1 cm. (about 1/4 inch). Their color is like that of the other lesions. The center part is covered with a thin and small scab. Here again the surrounding tissue shows no trace of redness, edema, or infection.

"Although these wounds appear superficial, drops of blood appeared before my very eyes in a quantity more remarkable than on the other wounds.

"When I examined them for the first time, around 9:00 o'clock in the evening, I removed from the surface of one of the wounds a cloth about the size of an ordinary handkerchief, completely soaked by bloody serum. I substituted another white handkerchief, so that in the morning I could observe the blood soaked up by it. I repeated my examination at about 7:00 o'clock, that is to say, about ten hours after the previous examination. I found this handkerchief, plus a new piece of cloth of equal size, placed over the wound by Padre Pio during the night, both completely soaked with the same bloody secretion. This loss of blood is substantial, continuous, and occurs for a long time.

"These things that I have described, in the palms and backs of the hands, in the soles and tops of the feet and in the chest region of the left side, are at this writing the only lesions that exist on the body of Padre Pio. The rest of his skin has a normal white color with all the normal, perfect characteristics of skin."

During this visit, the doctors witnessed more than the marvel of the stigmata. They also experienced a very conspicuous aroma, something which was to become a trademark of Padre Pio. Subsequently, thousands of people have experienced a variety of aromas. I will quote their testimony in a separate chapter.

One of Padre Pio's confreres described the wounds in Padre Pio's feet. "They were always swollen," he said, "very swollen, like melons, the right foot more than the left. I often thought that they were like Our Lord's feet on the cross. Probably the right foot crossed over the left and was more swollen, because the pressure of the right foot on the left would hold down the swelling."

In 1935, when Padre Pio's Mass still lasted over two hours, a spiritual daughter asked him: "Padre, don't you ever get tired, standing on your feet with those wounds?"

He replied: "I don't stand on my feet."

This answer puzzled her. "But Padre, I can see you stand on your feet. But then, if you are not standing on your feet, you must be on the cross."

He commented: "Is it only now that you are aware of it?"

As long as Padre Pio was able, he washed his wounds himself. But for almost the last three years of his life, he needed help. Padre Onorato had the dreadful honor of washing the wounds of his feet. But many other Capuchins, Padre Alessio, Padre Pellegrino, Brother Modestino, and Father Giuseppe Pio (Bill Martin, from Brooklyn, N.Y.), all of them tended his every need and had the chance to see the stigmata close up, repeatedly.

A few months before he died, Padre Pio's wounds became less bloody. A serum, rather than blood, oozed out of them. It seemed as though his system was running out of blood. For two months before his death, Padre Pio did not have to clean his wounds at all. In our chapter on his death, we will describe what happened to the wounds when he died.

One evening in early 1968, Padre Alessio helped Padre Pio as usual to prepare for bed. Padre Pio followed a regular pattern. He would wait for eight or ten minutes after retiring and then call Padre Alessio back into his room by ringing his bell. But this evening the bell was silent. Ten, twelve, fourteen minutes passed. Padre Alessio became alarmed.

He knocked on Padre Pio's door and said: "May I come in?"

"Come in, my son," Padre Pio pleaded. "Come in and help me." Padre Alessio found him sprawled half on the bed and half on the floor. His gloves, and the bandages which he also used under the gloves at that time, were strewn on the floor.

Padre Alessio lifted him onto the bed. Then Padre Pio sat on the edge of the bed and allowed Padre Alessio to wash his wounds.

"I saw his wounds," Padre Alessio told me, "and I cleaned them with the bandages which he used under his gloves. I had to use what was right there. The wounds were about as big as a penny. They were very deep, and they were covered with half-coagulated blood.

"I cleaned up the blood very hurriedly," Padre Alessio continued. "I was afraid every time I touched him. The wounds on the palms of his hands were completely closed up by the dried blood. The backs of his hands were all bloody. I cleaned them."

These eyewitnesses speak about Padre Pio quietly and unexcitedly, but they cannot completely conceal their bulldog loyalty to the man whom they call their Spiritual Father.

Padre Pio's slow and hesitating gait showed how agonizing were his wounds. He hobbled rather than walked. He probably would have been unable to walk at all, if it were not for his specially made sandals. They were styled like shoes, flexible, and made partially out of cloth. They were sent to him as a gift by friends in Switzerland.

One day a man from India visited Padre Pio. He was so overawed that he fell to his knees at Padre Pio's feet. Clasping his hands and bowing his head almost to the ground, in typical Indian fashion, he touched the Capuchin's stocking-covered feet. He didn't realize that those feet were dug with the same raw wounds that Padre Pio bore in his hands. Padre Pio screamed out in pain, until he checked himself and smiled on his well-intentioned admirer.

In addition to the three doctors whose reports we have quoted, another doctor has offered us some precious medical details of Padre Pio's life. He is Dr. Giuseppe Sala, Padre Pio's personal physician for ten years and Mayor of San Giovanni Rotondo.

I asked Dr. Sala if Padre Pio had ever had a blood test. The doctor answered affirmatively. When I asked him what the results were, he fielded my sophomoric question respectfully by asking me which of the many results I wanted to learn.

Several blood tests, the doctor told me, were conducted between 1958 and 1959 in the Casa Sollievo. He simplified his findings for me by saying:

"His blood showed normal characteristics, with the normal count of red and white cells. When the Padre was ill, his blood showed the changes that any normal person's blood would show. There was no anemia, in spite of his loss of blood. A person might think that he would be anemic and without any blood. Absolutely not! The fact is that his blood was normal. The only thing that was beyond comprehension was the nature of the wounds, which were not inflamed or infected. They were normal wounds, but not made by any type of instrument, gunshot, etc.

"They were a special kind of wounds, in that they did not have the capacity to heal as normal wounds do. They had characteristics that to a doctor are important. A doctor is interested in seeing if a wound is healing or if it is not going to heal. Padre Pio's wounds were beyond any anatomical classification. They were unique (sui generis)."

I took advantage of the chance to ask Dr. Sala about other medical questions, for example, Padre Pio's high temperatures which had shattered clinical thermometers. Dr. Sala, speaking only from his personal observation, remarked: "The temperature was normal when he was well. Sometimes, for various reasons, he had a fever, and his temperature reached 38 or 39.5 degrees C (100 or 103.5 degrees F). I personally have never witnessed a temperature over 40 degrees C (104 degrees F). If you refer to the reports of others who said that the thermometer used to break, I never witnessed this."

The most important question I asked Dr. Sala referred to the possibility of hysteria as an explanation for the existence of the stigmata. Dr. Sala responded immediately and emphatically:

"The wounds were not at all the result of hysteria. They were not caused by any irritation. They were physiological in their existence, but they were beyond any physiological explanation as to their cause. It is impossible for an hysterical person to produce holes in his hands or in his head. The existence of the wounds are independent of the character of Padre Pio, who was a gentle and calm person and not at all hysterical. The wounds were real and true wounds and not caused by irritation. They were not stimulated or induced by pricking. Although there were scratches or marks on his face, which he could have made himself, the stigmata were not self-made."

I asked Dr. Sala his opinion of Dr. Festa's medical reports. He responded: "Of the three doctors who examined Padre Pio's wounds, Dr. Festa was the most skeptical and critical. His examinations and his tests were severe. They were quite adequate, and I do not have anything to add to what he said. I could add some comments as an observer of a greater person by a lesser, but in the long run my comments would be same as those of Dr. Festa."

Of particular interest to Dr. Sala was the staggering workload which Padre Pio carried from morning to night, without a day off or vacation, for fifty years. He seemed to be unable to comprehend how Padre Pio could have endured such a pace.

Nor could he understand medically Padre Pio's physical ability to go on, with less than half of the minimum caloric intake necessary to sustain life. The doctor said: "Padre Pio averaged 500 to 600 calories a day, more or less, because under my care a few drops of whisky or brandy were added to his coffee. A normal person requires at least 1,400 to 1,600 calories a day." Until those few drops of brandy, his daily caloric intake was about 100!

The doctors estimated that the stigmata bled about a cup of blood a day, sometimes even more. Yet, Padre Pio was never anemic until the last months of his life. From 1918 on, blood didn't flow from the wounds. Rather, it oozed out. This bleeding never stopped, nor did the wounds ever become infected, although dark woolen socks and mittens could hardly have been conducive to good hygiene.

The only time Padre Pio's wounds could be seen publicly was during the Sacrifice of the Mass, when he removed his fingerless mittens. It was difficult even then to see the stigmata, because he tried to keep them covered as much as possible with the long sleeves of his habit and alb. But when he removed the mittens before Mass, coagulated blood showered down on the vesting table. People scampered for relics. I have seen scabs from his wounds, over one-eighth of an inch thick.

At night, he washed the wounds himself and then covered them with white, fingerless mittens. By morning, these mittens were soaked with blood.

During the day, he wore brown mittens, also fingerless. Around his chest he wore a sash from his waist to his armpits, which he changed two or three times every day. His lay friends supplied him with these materials. After they were used, the Capuchins wrapped them in plastic and stored them away, realizing their value for the future. Occasionally, a glove ended up in the hands of a layman.

Many years ago, a newspaper wrote an exposé of scandals in San Giovanni Rotondo, claiming that the Mafia had moved in and manufactured fake relics with chicken blood. If there was any substance to the newspaper article, the Capuchins in San Giovanni Rotondo could recall nothing of the sort.

The doctors themselves confessed their bewilderment over the stigmata. They were baffled, too, by the operations which Padre Pio had, one for hernia, and one for a cyst. The wounds from these operations healed normally, but the stigmata never healed.

The first of these operations was performed on October 5, 1925, eight years after he had received the stigmata permanently on his body. Dr. Festa has given us a lengthy account of the operation and what led up to it:

"On October 1, I was with Padre Pio in his room, exchanging pleasantries, when suddenly the good friar interrupted: 'I want to ask you a question. . . . Do me the favor of examining me. . . . For several years I have experienced sharp pains every once in awhile, which pierce my intestines. Now these pains come very frequently, and their intensity is atrocious. When I ascend the altar steps, I have to use extraordinary efforts to keep myself from fainting. Please examine me and prescribe some remedy that will relieve me and permit me to continue my priestly duties.'

"I examined him closely and found a voluminous hernia in the region of the right groin. . . . Adhesive peritonitis had set in, which was painful and disposed him to nausea and to vomiting.

"The functions of his heart, kidneys, and respiratory tracts now appeared to be very normal, more or less as they were several years ago when Dr. Bignami and I examined him.

". . . I knew that the best recommendation that I could make was to operate. The good Padre was not upset. He welcomed my verdict. He simply said: 'It's too bad that I didn't think of having you examine me before. Maybe I would have begged you to operate on me then.' "

The Casa Sollievo was not yet in existence. So all parties agreed that the operation should take place in the friary. When Dr. Festa had arrived in San Giovanni Rotondo a week earlier, he saw a Brother whitewashing the walls of a room, and joked with him that it would make a good operating room. "I never dreamed," Dr. Festa said later, "that it was being prepared for Padre Pio's operation."

A friend brought Dr. Festa's surgical instruments from Rome, and Dr. Angelo Merla arrived to assist him. Padre Fortunato, who had been in the medical corps during the war, also helped. A layman, Emanuele Brunatto, was stationed at the door as sentry.

Everything was ready for the operation — everything except the patient. He was busy hearing many confessions that morning. He also chanted a Requiem Mass for the deceased benefactors of the Capuchin Order, and gave Benediction of the Most Blessed Sacrament. Finally, at noon, he retired to the friary.

"We saw him approaching, walking very slowly," Dr. Festa reports. "He was pallid from the sustained fatigue of the morning and from the physical pain which the hernia and his stigmata caused him."

When Padre Pio entered the makeshift operating room, he emphatically refused any anesthetic. "If you chloroform me," he challenged Dr. Festa, "how could I keep you from inspecting the wound in my side? You see, I have reason not to take an anesthetic. Don't worry. When you're finished, you will find me in the same place where you put me in the beginning."

For at least a modicum of relief, Dr. Festa offered Padre Pio a drink of Benedictine. Padre Pio drank it right out of the bottle.

"Take a little more," the doctor urged.

"No, that's sufficient." Padre Pio answered. "Otherwise we risk an internal scuffle between the Benedictine and the Capuchin."

The operation lasted almost two hours. Padre Pio never complained. "Only once," Dr. Festa reported, "I saw two tears roll down his cheeks as he lay there and groaned: 'Jesus, pardon me if I don't know how to suffer as I should.' "

During the operation, everyone in the room heard an insect buzzing and scurried around to find it.

"It's not a fly," Padre Pio said. "It's a mosquito, there, up there, in the corner of the window," and he pointed at it.

While the doctor was putting in the stitches after the operation, a local veterinarian, Dr. Alessandro Giuva, tried to enter the room, but the stout guard Brunatto stopped him. Tempers rose and shouts were exchanged. Padre Pio heard the commotion and called out: "If you want to take my place, Alessandro, you can come in. The table is still warm."

Giuva blushed. He, too, had a hernia, but out of shame he had never mentioned it to anyone.

After the operation, Padre Pio was walked back to his room. There he collapsed, unconscious. Now Dr. Festa had his chance. "I confess that during this period," the doctor admitted, "I took advantage of his condition and explored the wound over his heart, which I had reported on five years earlier. I was able to observe the same characteristics that I had noted then.

"For the love of truth and exactness, I must add only that the soft skin of the scab, which covered the wound on the left side two inches from under the nipple in the preceding examination, has now fallen off. This wound now appears fresh and of a vermilion color, in the form of a cross, and with short but conspicuous rays which spread out from the edges of the wound."

Four days after the operation, the doctor removed the bandage. Everything was perfect. There was no swelling or redness. He removed some of the stitches immediately, and the rest of them two days later. "I considered him cured," he said. "After a brief convalescence, Padre Pio resumed his activities with greater vigor and without tiring himself as in the past."

Two years later, Dr. Festa again operated on Padre Pio, this time for a cyst on the side of his neck. Dr. Merla again assisted him. "We already knew how he thought," Dr. Festa said, "so I didn't insist on any form of anesthesia."

The cyst was about as big as a pigeon's egg. The operation and the stitching of the wound lasted half an hour. The patient showed no reaction at all. At the end, Dr. Festa asked him: "Didn't you have any pain?"

"Certainly, I did," Padre Pio answered.

"Then why didn't you move your head or complain?"

"What good would it do me to move or to cry? I would have embarrassed you, your work would have taken longer, and my pain would have been worse. So you see, by not complaining, I was looking after my own interests."

In spite of the pain from the operation, Padre Pio did not take off one day from his ministry. The next morning he offered Mass and heard confessions as though nothing had happened.

Dr. Festa carefully observed his physical condition. "Within the fifth and sixth days," he reported, "as it was also after the hernia operation, the incision was perfectly healed, and I removed the stitches. But the five wounds of the hands, the feet and the side have never healed for the past forty-five years. This fact is a riddle which the rationalists, the psychologists, and the exponents of hysteria have to solve."

CHAPTER 7

Rumors and Riots

When word has spread that the stigmata have appeared, the Catholic Church does not immediately sing Alleluia and ring the church bells. The Catholic Church is a wise old Mother with experience stretching back for almost two millennia. If the Vatican should decide to investigate a claim of the stigmata, or if miracles are claimed, on the Vatican level the case is looked into by the Sacred Congregation for the Doctrine of the Faith, previously called the Holy Office.

The Holy Office began its investigation by restricting Padre Pio from offering Mass in public. To this decree, almost every one of the three thousand men, women and children of San Giovanni responded by staging a demonstration in front of the friary. On this occasion, the civil authorities were able to disperse the crowd without incident. They petitioned Rome, and after fifteen days obtained a suspension of the decree. But that was the end only of a battle, not of the war.

Since September 6, 1919, rumors had been bandied about, with some foundation, that Padre Pio was to be transferred. The townsfolk had been observing frequent visits by strangers, whom they strongly suspected of skulduggery. Also, newspapers around the world were carrying feature articles on Padre Pio, and an influx of visitors had already begun. The people of San Giovanni Rotondo feared that if tourism increased, they would never be able to get near their good shepherd.

They responded to these new threats with typical Italian verve. On October 14, 1920, they rallied in the piazza of the town, brandishing clubs and pitchforks and guns, swords and bayonets, which many had smuggled out of the army after the war. Somehow, the rally broke into a riot, and before peace was restored, fourteen people lay dead and eighty injured.

The riot encouraged the Holy Office to enforce its decision to transfer Padre Pio. They judged that if the cause of the *chiasso,* the trouble, were removed, the commotion would subside. Mayor Morcaldi complained: "The ecclesiastical authority had not abandoned its past proposal. No account seemed to be taken of the dangers involving the preservation of public order."

Maybe the mayor was right in saying that the Vatican didn't seem to take account of the dangers involved in their decisions. On the other hand, we must keep everything in historical focus.

We are looking back over a period of Padre Pio's fifty years in San Giovanni Rotondo. The Church in the 1920s and 1930s was looking ahead, not back. We have the advantage of hindsight with which to judge the prudence of the Church. We know now that Padre Pio was a man of God. The Church at that time was trying to learn the facts.

Also, think of the other problems which the Vatican was facing. The savage military juggernaut of international Communism had already torn Russia apart. Spain, a whole Catholic nation, was going through a blood-bath. The Church in Mexico was convulsed by the persecution by Calles. Hitler's Nazism and Mussolini's Fascism were not games which little boys were playing. And so on, all around the globe. Without minimizing Rome's concern for "little people," in fairness we must remember that other events of the day were closer to center stage than those in San Giovanni Rotondo.

How did Padre Pio respond to all of this? According to Morcaldi, in his history of San Giovanni Rotondo: "Padre Pio passed his days serenely in prayer and penance, unconcerned with the tempest which seemed to be brewing around him."

Padre Pio's composure during this imbroglio was indeed remarkable. There was a priest, for example, who had maliciously slandered Padre Pio, causing widespread scandal. Then, for other reasons, the priest was arrested and jailed.

Upon his release, he felt the need to visit Padre Pio. Padre Pio, like the father of the Prodigal Son in the Gospel, didn't wait for the priest to approach him. "Padre Pio ran out to greet him," Padre Michaelangelo said. "Padre Pio got down on his knees before him, kissed his hand and embraced him as the dearest friend. And this was the one who had written a libelous booklet against him!"

Further on in this book I will describe in detail the fabulous Casa Sollievo della Sofferenza, the Home for the Relief of Suffering, which Padre Pio built for the poor of southern Italy. He told Padre Michaelangelo: "Do you see that Home? You know the suffering it has caused me. Well, if to save a brother someone would say to me: 'Place a bomb under it and blow that Home to smithereens,' I would not hesitate one single moment to do so. To save souls! And I save them, not with force, not with condemnation, not with punishment, not with hate. I do so with love, with prayer, with a blessing, with an embrace."

Again, the Vatican played its hand on June 2, 1922,

through a letter to the Superior General of the Capuchin Order.

The Father General was ordered to tell the local superior in San Giovanni Rotondo "to keep Padre Pio under observation." Furthermore, "all singularity and noise were to be avoided." Padre Pio was forbidden to celebrate Mass at a fixed hour. His Mass schedule had to be irregular, and he was to offer Mass "preferably very early in the morning, and in private, and he may not give his blessing to the people, and on no account may he show anyone the stigmata, which he is said to bear, nor may he speak about them or allow them to be kissed."

In the same decree, Padre Pio was ordered to choose another spiritual director instead of Padre Benedetto "with whom he must break off all communication, even by letter."

Directives one after the other were issued in rapid fire by the Holy Office. On May 31, 1923 the following notice appeared in *L'Osservatore Romano*:

"The Supreme Congregation of the *Holy Office,* in care of the Faith and its defense, after an investigation into the matters attributed to Padre Pio of Pietrelcina of the Capuchin Friars Minor, residing in the friary of San Giovanni Rotondo, in the diocese of Foggia (in reality, Manfredonia) *declares*, after the aforementioned investigation, *that there is nothing supernatural* (all italics theirs) in these matters and exhorts the faithful to comply with this accordingly."

Substantially the same statement was reissued on July 6, 1924; April 23, 1926; July 11, 1926, and June 9, 1931.

Back and forth for four years, from 1919 to 1923, the tides of peace and crisis ebbed and flowed. A mob would storm the Capuchin friary, and Padre Pio would calm them down.

The order previously given by Rome restricted Padre Pio to Mass in an inside chapel. However, laymen were allowed to attend. On June 17, 1923 that loophole was plugged. Henceforth, his Mass might be offered only "in one chapel inside of the friary, without the participation of any outsider."

Padre Ignazio, the local superior in office for only a few months, feared another uprising of the people. He went to Foggia to convince his Provincial Superior of the dangers of following the order of June 17. The answer to his appeal: "The orders must be obeyed." That decision occasioned what Mayor Morcaldi calls "the magnificent demonstration (*superba manifestazione*)" of June 25.

Again the people rallied in the town square, and threatened to burn the homes of some local priests who they thought were behind the decrees.

"If they try to transfer Padre Pio," the mayor pledged, "I'll resign and fight with you as a citizen." His words quieted them down. The crowd then proceeded peacefully to the church.

"It was an extraordinary show of faith and love for Padre Pio," the mayor wrote in his history of the town. "The streets, the piazza, the church were jammed. The crowd surrounded Padre Pio, who came down to the church to sing the Te Deum. The superior, Padre Ignazio, promised that in the morning Padre Pio would return to work among the people. The crowd cheered. When the religious services were over, the people knelt in the square in front of the church and along the street, to get Padre Pio's blessing as he stood at the church entrance."

As far as we know, Padre Ignazio had solved this problem in his own way, contrary to the decision which he had just received from his Father Provincial in Foggia. We are not aware of any reversal of the ban by the higher authorities in the Church. Probably he felt that only he knew all the circumstances, especially the seriousness of the situation. Whether his action was right or wrong, he restored the peace, and on June 26, 1923, as he promised, Padre Pio was restored to his flock.

The people of San Giovanni Rotondo then formed a

new committee, presided over by Mayor Morcaldi. On July 1, the committee went to Rome, where they were received kindly by two Cardinals. But Cardinal Gasparri offered them little hope. He told them that at the moment "the events at San Giovanni Rotondo are not of such importance that there is need of special intervention by the Holy See." Presumably by "special intervention" the Cardinal meant "additional intervention." The Holy See had already intervened in the recent past.

The roller coaster ride of war and peace continued. Finally the moment came when the Vatican decided that "special intervention" was imperative. This time the Vatican was determined to transfer Padre Pio.

The Capuchin Minister General in Rome, Father Joseph Anthony, summoned a priest, Father Luigi Festa (no relative of Dr. Festa), and commissioned him to act as his delegate. "The roof is going to fall in on you!" Father Joseph told Father Luigi. "You will have to follow the orders of the supreme authority. Padre Pio is in your hands. Bring him from San Giovanni Rotondo and present him to the Provincial of the Marches of Ancona until further notice. . . . Deliver this decree to Padre Pio, and when the time is right, act!"

To prevent a recurrence of 1920, which everyone remembered, Father Joseph urged General DeBono, the Director of Public Safety, to guarantee the safe escort of Padre Pio from San Giovanni Rotondo to Ancona.

"We can safeguard Padre Pio's passage," General DeBono promised, "but somebody's blood will probably be shed. The Prefect of Foggia has promised to help, but he said that we surely will have to walk over dead bodies."

The noose was tightening. On August 7, 1923, Padre Luigi arrived at San Giovanni Rotondo and called Padre Pio to his room. When Padre heard the decision of the Father General, he bowed his head, threw open his arms and answered: "I am ready to follow your wishes. Let us leave right away. When I am with my superior, I am with God." It was midnight.

"You want to leave now?" Padre Luigi asked, taken aback. "Where shall we go?"

Padre Pio answered him: "I don't know, but I shall go with you whenever you tell me to go."

So choked with emotion was Padre Luigi that he could only tell Padre Pio to wait until he received further instructions from Rome.

In the meantime, the hackles again were up on the backs of the people of the town. With their uncanny sense, they learned on August 8 that Padre Luigi had arrived, and they smelled blood. They labeled him "the hangman's assistant chosen by the authorities of the Church to strike the blow," and again they stormed up the *Viale Cappuccini,* the main road leading to the friary.

Mayor Morcaldi met Padre Pio at the church. They embraced, but this time there was something different in their *bacio.* "It was an embrace," the mayor recalled, "that indicated a farewell."

The next day, August 10, 1923, was the thirteenth anniversary of Padre Pio's ordination to the priesthood. This year the people celebrated it by posting a 24-hour guard at every door of the friary. They vowed to die rather than allow their beloved Padre to be shanghaied.

Nobody in the crowd paid any special attention to a wild-eyed young man named Donato. But at the end of Benediction of the Blessed Sacrament, he stalked into the sacristy, whipped out a gun, and leveled it at Padre Pio. "Dead or alive," he shouted, "You're going to stay with us here in this village."

Immediately the people surrounded him and disarmed him. The violence of this act sobered the crowd, including Donato himself, who begged Padre Pio's pardon. Everyone went home, except Padre Pio and the guards. The guards remained at the doors. Padre Pio went to the chapel. There, before Jesus in the Blessed Sacrament, he wrote a letter:

"Lord, what do these people want of us? My life is in the hands of the young people of this district and my superiors. Lord, you saw what happened this evening, the young man and how he was armed. But you could also see into his heart, and so you know his intentions were good. You know his name and trade, Jesus. You know what it is to be killed for the sake of love. Donato wanted to kill for love, too, Lord. You never condemned love. Because of this I ask you to forgive him, because you love him as I do. He is a bricklayer. He uses picks, shovels and spades. He works with lime and brick, and with these rough materials he can fashion a skilled trade. Maybe it is because of this that he doesn't like crude things. Now he is sleeping peacefully. Jesus, don't let nightmares trouble his sleep, nor bad memories torment him during the days. Let him rest peacefully, and send your blessing down on the people of San Giovanni Rotondo.

"What tomorrow may bring, I do not know. I do not know where my superiors will send me. I, your faithful son of holy obedience, will obey without a murmur, since so much depends on me.

"I will post this. I know my final end will come in believing, knowing, the intentions of my dear and chosen people of San Giovanni to keep me with them, if not alive then at least dead. I hope that the civil and legal authorities will not apply the law again to those who have tried to harm me. I have always loved everyone and pardoned everyone, and I don't want to die before having pardoned whoever tried to kill me.

"I have written this in front of the Blessed Sacrament in my full senses and trembling with love for God and for all my brothers in Christ.
"San Giovanni Rotondo, 10th of August, 1923
"Padre Pio, Capuchin, from Pietrelcina"

Padre Pio continued in prayer:

"Jesus, these people, what do they want of me? If I knew, couldn't I do something for them? I would not ask you, but I know they want me living or dead. Lord, living I do not count. Do not dispose of me, because dead I am worth even less. Living I am not worth anything. I am only an encumbrance. They will put me where they want, in an obscure room where I will give the least annoyance possible. But if I were dead, my body would lie harmless. The people of San Giovanni want my body. I don't know why, nor do I know what they would do with a dead body, and I don't want to feel that I deceived them. And so Lord, not knowing what to do, I have asked you that my bones may be laid in this ground inhabited by the people whom I recommend to you with love when I am praying to you. Perhaps you are smiling or replying. Perhaps you are not saying anything."

Two days later, Padre Pio wrote another letter, to Mayor Francesco Morcaldi, pleading with him not to interfere with the decisions which were made by the Church:

"The developments of the last few days have deeply moved me and immensely preoccupied me. They make me dread the fact that I should be the involuntary cause of disturbances to my beloved citizenry. I pray God to dispel this misfortune and to send me any mortification He wishes. However, since the decision of my transfer has been given, I beg you to set about with every means at your disposal, to comply with the will of my superiors which is the will of God and which I intend to obey blindly.

"I shall always remember this generous people in my poor prayers, begging for them as a sign of my love for them, peace and prosperity. Unable to do anything else, I express my desire, as long as my superiors do not oppose it, to have my bones put in a tiny corner of the ground here.

"Respectfully yours in our sweet Lord
"Padre Pio of Pietrelcina
"August 12, 1923"

While these threads were being raveled, the appeal of Father Luigi to Father Joseph, the General Superior, was still pending. Then was given the dramatic and unexpected response by the Holy Office, dated August 17, 1923: *"Ordo suspendatur donec aliter* — the transfer order is suspended until further notice!"

The suspension of the transfer orders brought another lull in the storm. But the storm was far from over. That would come only with the poor man's death.

The Holy See had the fixed idea that peace could be restored by Padre Pio's transfer. On April 7, 1931, the transfer syndrome again emerged, shadowed as usual by more riots.

Up the hill the people marched again. This time they didn't stop at the door. They broke it down. Men and women surged through the cloister. The women couldn't care less about the excommunication which they incurred by violating the monastic enclosure. There was an "enemy" in the friary who was going to remove their Padre, and they demanded that this enemy be handed over to them.

Padre Raffaele, the superior, tried to assuage them. Yes, he admitted, there was a visiting priest in the friary, but he would not take Padre Pio away.

"You are saying that under obedience," they shouted back at him. "You're lying."

"We are sons of St. Francis," Padre Raffaele retorted, "and we will give hospitality to other priests in our house. You can be sure that he will leave in the morning."

Seeing that he was getting nowhere with the angry crowd, Padre Raffaele summoned Padre Pio, who assured them that he would not be transferred. Padre Pio they believed, but they watched the situation very closely.

"I'll take care of the enemy," Alessandro Giuva boasted, the veterinarian who had walked in on Padre Pio's hernia operation. "In the morning I'll escort him myself to Foggia." Again an armistice was achieved.

On June 9, 1931 the Vatican moved again. Padre Pio was instructed "to desist from all activity except the celebration of Mass." To prevent a repetition of the past, the restriction was added that nobody except the servers may attend the Mass. "God's will be done," was Padre Pio's only comment. It was the Feast of Corpus Christi.

During this period of almost absolute solitary confinement, he was restricted to his room and forbidden all contact with seculars. He was given a schedule which allowed two hours in the morning for Mass. Then prayers in the oratory till noon. Then one hour of study in the library, and prayer in the afternoon after Vespers, and then more prayer until midnight.

This imprisonment, as Padre Pio called it, lasted two

full years. How he reacted to it is described by Padre Agostino, his new director after Rome forbade him to contact Padre Benedetto. In his *Diario,* Padre Agostino wrote:

"In the beginning of March (1931) I went to San Giovanni Rotondo for a few hours. . . . His spirit is calm, and he continues onward in holy obedience. . . .

"On July 1, I went to San Giovanni Rotondo and chatted with our dear Padre Pio for an hour. The order from the Holy Office depriving him of all his priestly powers, except for the right to celebrate Mass in private, had arrived on June 12, 1931. As a result, I found Padre Pio exceedingly depressed. Hardly were we alone in his cell when he began to cry. Although deeply affected by this, I was able to quell my own emotions and let him cry for some time. Afterwards we talked. Dear Padre Pio told me that he was quite affected by this unexpected trial. . . . Padre Pio answered, 'I never thought that this would happen,' . . .

"On July 24, 1931, I returned to San Giovanni Rotondo. . . . 'How do you spend your days?' I questioned him. 'I study as much as I can, and then I annoy my brothers,' he answered. 'How is this possible?' I asked. 'As always, I tell them jokes, and the jokes are even worse than before.' Then, changing his tone, he added, 'The first days of this terrible trial were very hard on me, but then God gave me strength. After that, I was able to adapt myself to this new way of life. May Jesus be praised!'

". . . He added, 'Meanwhile, for the present Jesus is silent. He makes Himself neither seen nor heard. It is just like living in agony. But let His will be done.' . . . His stigmata continues to bleed, especially the wound in his side. I was able to steal one of the handkerchiefs that he had used to cover the wound in his side!

"On September 24, . . . I smelled the perfume in Padre Pio's cell. I don't know how many times I have entered his room, spoken to him and touched handkerchiefs that have been soaked with his blood without ever before smelling this perfume. I do not have words to describe the scene; but it is sweet, pleasant, pure. . . . I must say that I am capable of smelling only a strong fragrance. My sense of smell was damaged, undoubtedly because from the time I was a child until I was twenty-two I suffered greatly from continuous nosebleeds. Only now can I perceive the fragrance that is said to come from Padre Pio and anything he touches. Even today, as I write this, seven days after my visit to Padre Pio, I am aware of the perfume. . . .

". . . His soul is ready and always willing to accept the divine plan.

"Padre Pio prays and suffers . . . suffers and prays."

On Christmas Day, in 1932, Padre Pio took five hours to offer his three Masses.

In the tempests and in the doldrums, which ranged from San Giovanni Rotondo to Rome and back again, everyone heard the haunting, hollow echo of the massacre of 1920. On this one point everyone was agreed, that no more blood should be shed.

But again the rumors began to fly, and again the patience of the people reached its elastic limit. The mayor of San Giovanni Rotondo washed his hands of any responsibility and wrote to the Provincial Government in Foggia: "Who will be responsible for the people who will die if Padre Pio is transferred?"

The Prefect in Foggia in turn also disclaimed any responsibility for possible bloodshed and contacted the national government in Rome. There Mussolini's office continued the concatenation by contacting the Vatican. In that court of last appeal, Pope Pius XI stepped in and ordered the Holy Office to reverse its ban. The Pope said to Padre Pio's Archbishop: "I have not been badly disposed toward Padre Pio (*Io non sono stato maldisposito del Padre Pio*), but I have been badly informed about Padre Pio (*ma io sono stato malinformato del Padre Pio*)."

Now Padre Pio was again allowed to celebrate Mass in the church. A year later, on March 25, 1934, he was allowed to hear confessions of men, and on May 12, 1934, confessions of women.

The rumors of a transfer behind him, Padre Pio's daily cross took another form. On August 3, 1952, *L'Osservatore Romano* published a decree of the Holy Office which condemned certain books about Padre Pio because they were published without the necessary revision, and without the approval of the Church. Express mention was made that this decision did not imply "any condemnation of Padre Pio, or of any authors of the books."

L'Osservatore Romano is an official newspaper of the Vatican. Legal matters are not officially promulgated through it, but rather through the *Acta Apostolicae Sedis*. Very significantly, the decree of the Holy Office never appeared in the *Acta*.

Still, the action of the Holy Office stirred up a hornet's nest and threw an even darker cloud of suspicion over Padre Pio.

During these most recent events, just as in previous decades, Padre Pio's only defense was "no defense." He gave the same silent, blind, and unquestioning obedience to his superiors which he had given all through his life.

But he was not without emotion, and he was not unmindful of the past. No doubt his thoughts turned back to the time when he penned these words to his spiritual director: "In the decisions of authority I find my only support. This alone holds me up in the dark way in which I find myself."

How vividly he must have recalled his first leap into the darkness of obedience to the Pope. It was during World War I. Pope Benedict XV had begged the whole Church to offer prayers and sacrifices for the world.

Even before the Pope's request was publicized, Padre Pio did exactly what the Pope had asked. And what a sacrifice he made! "I offered my whole being to Our Lord," Padre Pio wrote in 1918, "for the same intentions of the Holy Father. As soon as I did that, I felt I was returning to a hard prison, and I heard the door of the prison bang loudly as it closed behind me. I felt that I was fastened with very hard shackles and was about to die on the spot. Ever since, I have felt that I was in hell."

CHAPTER 8

At Mass

From the minute Padre Pio awakened, even if it was in the middle of the night, he was like a race horse in the starting gate until he could begin Mass. "What time is it?" he would ask Padre Onorato at 12:30 in the morning.

"It's 12:30. It's still early," Padre Onorato would reassure him.

"Remember," Padre Pio would insist, "don't let me be late. I must be up at 1:00 o'clock."

"He couldn't be late," Padre Onorato explained to us, "because at 1:00 o'clock he was already awake. He would say: 'Help me to get up. What am I doing in this bed?'"

From 1:30 to 4:00 o'clock he would sit in his little armchair, clutching his rosary. The motion of his lips betrayed the devotion of his heart as he prepared for Mass by praying the rosary.

At 4:00 o'clock he would go downstairs to the sacristy and continue his preparation for Mass. All during the next hour he would continue to ask what time it was. "There is still time," his brethren kept telling him.

His reaction was immediate: "What! Four o'clock

struck ages ago. Quickly! Quickly! Help me to put on my vestments for Mass.''

"His anxiety was a real torment," Padre Onorato told us. "He pressed us more and more. As soon as he had put on his vestments, I had to make him sit down, so he would not get too tired. As we waited, he would call out again: 'Onorato! Onorato!' I would immediately respond, but all he had to say was: 'Hurry up! At 5:00 o'clock I must be at the altar.' "

Padre Eusebio remarked that it was a trial to see him in that condition, that only the thought of obedience could calm him down and force him to wait for the time of Mass. But when the time actually came to begin Mass, he would become calm. His face would light up.

Sometimes as Padre Pio approached the altar, he would tremble. "Why do you tremble like that," Cleonice Morcaldi, a native of San Giovanni Rotondo, once asked him. "Is it because you have to suffer?"

"No," he answered her, "it isn't because of what I have to suffer, but because of what I have to offer. Don't you realize the great mystery of the Mass? We priests are the butchers who slaughter Jesus the victim, to offer Him to our heavenly Father in payment for our sins."

Padre Pio almost always cried throughout the Mass. The same lady asked him why he cried, and he told her: "I don't want to shed small tears. I want to shed a flood of tears. Don't you see the great mystery of the Mass?"

Everyone I spoke to told me that it was impossible to describe what Padre Pio's Mass was like.

"His face was transfigured, literally," they told me.

One of his biographers, Maria Winowska, tried to capture something of this when she wrote: "The Capuchin's face which a few moments before had seemed to me jovial and affable was literally transfigured. . . . Fear, joy, sorrow, agony or grief. . . . I could follow the mysterious dialogue on (his) features. Now he protests, shakes his head in denial and waits for the reply. His entire body was frozen in mute supplication. . . .

"Suddenly great tears welled from his eyes, and his shoulders, shaken with sobs, seemed bowed beneath a crushing weight. . . . Between himself and Christ there was no distance. . . .

"I defy those who have been at San Giovanni Rotondo to attend Mass as mere spectators. . . .

"One Friday I saw him panting, oppressed as a wrestler at bay trying in vain with swift tosses of the head to shake off some obstacle which prevented him from uttering the words of Consecration. It eventually resembled a single combat from which he emerged victorious but broken. On other occasions after the Sanctus great drops of sweat poured from his forehead, bathing his face which was distorted with sobs. Here was truly the man of sorrow at grips with the agony."

Father Donan (Danny) Hickey, now a Capuchin missionary in the Marianas Islands, describes his impression when as a GI during World War II he saw Padre Pio at Mass. "At the Consecration, if his voice was loud enough to be heard, the words came out rough-sounding and harsh, as if he were in great pain or anguish; he often seemed to be crying as he pronounced them. When he made the first genuflection, he remained a comparatively long time on his knees, staring intently at the Host; and when he tried to rise to his feet again, it was apparently with enormous effort, so much so that I often wondered if he was going to be able to stand at all. And the subsequent elevation of the Host required another tremendous physical effort."

In the early years of his priesthood, Padre Pio's Mass lasted about three hours. He didn't dillydally. He took so long because he was in ecstasy. He once said that in this absorption in God, especially at the Consecration of the Mass, he saw everyone who had asked his prayers. He told his friends that they could always reach him when he was at the altar. He saw them, actually, in his gaze on God.

In the beginning of his ministry, people lost patience with him because of the time he took for Mass. Sometimes Don Pannullo, the pastor of the church in Pietrelcina, would give him a mental command to continue Mass, and Padre Pio would respond immediately.

In the 1950s, Padre Pio's Mass lasted about an hour-and-a-half on weekdays, and two-and-a-quarter to two-and-a-half hours on Sundays. In the late 1960s, his Mass lasted about an hour.

During World War II, tens of thousands of GI's visited Padre Pio, and if possible they attended his Mass. On one occasion a group of U.S. Army officers visited him. They stood at ramrod attention during the entire Mass. When Mass was over, they continued to stand at attention, as though they were transfixed.

When the Italian Bishops authorized the change in the Mass from Latin to Italian, Padre Pio asked for and received permission to continue using Latin. He asked this permission not because he resisted the change. He had proven often enough that he saw the will of God in every command of his superiors.

He asked permission to retain the Latin because it was nearly impossible for him to change. He was almost eighty years old at the time and was almost blind. He was so ill that doctors could not understand how he continued to live. He had already received permission to substitute the Masses of the Blessed Mother and for the Dead in place of the prescribed Mass formula. Nobody can legitimately accuse him of resisting the changes in the Church.

In January, 1968, he received another permission, to remain seated during Mass. He continued to follow all the rubrics, but he had to rest his elbows on the altar. He did not have the strength to lift his arms.

There is no doubt that Padre Pio identified himself

with Jesus during the offering of the Mass. "You had to see him to understand this," people told me. Everyone could see Padre Pio's identification with Jesus. But there were three people who saw more than a priest who was completely absorbed in the holy Sacrifice.

One of them was Cleonice Morcaldi. It was her compassion which occasioned the most severe shock of her life. She had made a white linen undershirt for Padre Pio. He returned it to her three days later and asked her to please wash it.

She brought it home and opened the package. "Madonna!" she gasped. "It is one flagellation." It was splattered with blood from top to bottom, from front to back. Miss Morcaldi could not resist mentioning to Padre Pio what she had seen. "Padre," she said, "you are one big wound from head to foot."

He answered: "Isn't that for our glory? If there is no room for new wounds on my body, we will add wound upon wound." On the tunic, which is now kept in the Capuchin archives, you can see exactly that, blood upon blood.

"Padre," she cried, thoroughly choked with emotion, "you are the carnage of your own body."

"What you see," Padre Pio told her, "is not there just for the sake of pain. I am made out of flesh and blood like you. But I offer my pain to God because of the reward it gives me. It isn't only God who sends me pain. It is also I who ask for suffering for God's glory, for the salvation of all mankind and for freedom for the souls in Purgatory. What more can I ask?"

Another person who received a similar shock treatment was a young man who had been dating a girl from San Giovanni Rotondo. As a condition for their marriage, she demanded that he visit Padre Pio.

One morning the young man attended Padre Pio's Mass and stood in the back of the church. For several days following, he returned to the church to attend Mass.

After a week he broke down and cried. Padre Pio saw him and said: "Thank God for what you have seen, and don't tell anyone. God's secrets should be kept hidden in your heart."

"Yes," the young man agreed, realizing that Padre Pio knew what he had seen. "I have seen you on the altar, crowned with thorns, first with a triple crown of thorns, and then with something like a bonnet of thorns."

Padre Pio repeated, "Go home, thank God, and tell no one." But the young man told his fiancée. He told her that each morning at Mass he had seen Padre Pio, his head crowned with thorns, his face covered with blood, but with a serene, beautiful expression on his face.

The young lady could not resist telling her friends in San Giovanni Rotondo what she had heard. Miss Morcaldi, a daily visitor to the church, asked Padre Pio if the story were true.

"Do you have any doubt?" Padre Pio scolded: "You are like St. Thomas."

For many years the memory of this incident disturbed Miss Morcaldi. Finally she questioned Padre Pio again. "Padre," she asked, "that crown of thorns. . . . Do you wear it throughout the Mass?"

He replied: "You certainly want to know too much. Yes, before and after Mass, the crown that God has put on me is never taken off."

Perhaps this answer sheds some light on another phenomenon that the Capuchins at San Giovanni Rotondo have accepted simply as a matter of fact without attempting an explanation. During Mass, the friars who assisted Padre Pio always kept a supply of handkerchiefs at hand and frequently wiped the abundant perspiration from his brow and face. On one occasion, however, Padre Pellegrino smelled not perspiration but blood on the handkerchief. The smell was so strong that he thought he would throw up.

Padre Pellegrino gave eleven of these handkerchiefs

to Padre Onorato to be saved. Each article, as usual, was identified and numbered. Later, when the handkerchiefs were to be placed in separate plastic envelopes and transferred to another box, blood was discovered on three of them. One handkerchief was very heavily stained with blood, one was lightly stained with blood, and the third had bloodstains which reminded the Capuchins of three tears of blood, each about the size of a quarter.

In the interest of recording the whole truth about Padre Pio, fantastic as it may seem, we must record the experience of yet another person who witnessed his living conformity to the suffering Jesus.

Laurino Costa is the head cook at the Casa Sollievo, Padre Pio's hospital. When he first arrived in San Giovanni Rotondo, he was slow in conceding any claim of sanctity to Padre Pio, in spite of the amazing "coincidences" which had led Laurino to stay in that town.

"When I came to San Giovanni Rotondo in 1956," he told me, "I had some doubt that Padre Pio really was a saint. Yes, I admitted, he might be a very distinctive person, but a saint, no! For three years I had such doubts. I never expressed them to anyone, not even to my wife."

One day Laurino went to the church for confession. A priest urged him: "Hurry, Laurino! If you hurry, you will be the first one today to go to confession."

He entered the sacristy, where Padre Pio heard the men's confessions. There he saw Padre Pio, a deep cross slashed across his forehead, his face covered with blood.

"I began to tremble from fright," Laurino said. "I called to him, but he didn't answer me. He just stared at me. And there was that cross, with blood flowing from it."

Instinctively, Laurino reached into his pocket for his handkerchief, to wipe the blood from Padre Pio's face. But his hand froze there. He could not move. The two men just stared at each other.

Almost ten minutes passed. "Padre! Padre!" Laurino called, beginning to feel faint. The Padre heaved a deep sigh. Then *Padre Pio* began to confess *Laurino's* sins and gave him absolution.

With that, Padre Pio began to recover a little, and he said to Laurino: "Well, Laurino, when did you make your last confession?"

"Nine days ago," Laurino answered. Padre Pio then repeated Laurino's sins again and gave him absolution. Then the cross on his forehead disappeared.

"I didn't say a word," Laurino recalled. "I just got up very slowly. As I left the sacristy, I let out a loud shriek and began to cry."

By this time the sacristy was filled with people waiting to go to confession. They asked Laurino what was the matter, thinking that Padre Pio had denied him absolution.

For three days and nights Laurino cried. He could not rid his memory of the awful scene which he had witnessed. At times it kept him from falling asleep until 2:30 in the morning.

Frantic for relief, Laurino turned to Padre Clemente and asked him what he should say and do. "Ask Padre Pio," was Padre Clemente's simple answer.

But Laurino couldn't find the courage even to enter the church, much less approach Padre Pio with a question like that. He couldn't eat or sleep. He was sure that he was losing his mind.

"I worked and I wept," he said. "I worked and I wept. I prayed and I wept continually."

Finally, one day after work, as Laurino walked slowly toward his home, he resolved to have it out with Padre Pio once and for all. He took a few steps toward the friary, but again he lost courage. He could not go on. He turned away. But again he found heart and reversed his field. He reached the friary, where he saw Padre Pio standing at the door, as if waiting for him. His heart leaped. He cried aloud and was unable to move.

"Come, come, Laurino," Padre Pio said gently. "What is the matter? What has happened?"

Finally Laurino found his voice and stammered: "Padre, tell me, why did you make me see you like that? Is it perhaps I who make you suffer so?"

Padre Pio replied: "What a dunce you are! It was a grace which God wanted to give you."

As Laurino and I sat quietly at his kitchen table and Laurino recalled this incident, he said: "This happened because I didn't believe in his sanctity. After that experience, woe to anyone who would dare to touch Padre Pio. I would scratch his eyes out with my two fingers."

CHAPTER 9

Ministry at San Giovanni Rotondo

A dozen Capuchins and laymen clustered around Padre Pio in the friary garden as he regaled them with one of his favorite anecdotes.

"Two men from the backwoods had just heard about the invention of the train," he told them.

" 'Let's take a ride,' one of the men said to his friend, and they entered the train station.

" 'Where do you want to go?' the ticket seller asked.

" 'What business is it of yours?' they answered indignantly."

On and on the story went, Padre Pio magnifying every detail to epic proportions.

"The train roared into a tunnel, and the men were terrified.

" 'Where are we going?' one asked.

" 'I think we're going into hell,' his friend replied.

" 'Don't worry,' his companion said. 'We have round trip tickets!' "

A man who had visions of Jesus and Mary, and whose body bore the stigmata of Jesus Christ, might be the last person you would imagine telling jokes. If people could learn of Padre Pio's sense of humor, maybe the Christian virtue of his joy would replace the Hollywood image of a Franciscan as a Sad Sack, with cowl (hood) up, hands in sleeves, eyes cast down, and somber as a corpse.

A dowager-type lady visited San Giovanni Rotondo, anxious to meet Padre Pio. She pressed Brother Modestino for help. He suggested that she wait in the passageway between the church and the friary. When Padre Pio came along, she didn't recognize him.

"Where is the holy Father?" she asked him.

Padre Pio, playing on her words, answered, "The Holy Father is in Rome."

"No," she insisted, "I mean the holy Father here."

"Yes, I know, but the Holy Father is in Rome," Padre Pio repeated, as he walked with her along the corridor to the front office.

"Well, I'm sorry," she said. "I thought I could meet him here." The woman and the holy Father went their separate ways.

"Padre Pio not only had a sense of humor," one of his confreres attested, "but he had a very refined sense of humor. I'd call it wit. He was jovial, always joking without being silly. He wasn't ever silly."

One day an elegantly dressed lady visited Padre Pio. Her ruffled dress and flowery hat contrasted with the stark simplicity of the Italian ladies of San Giovanni Rotondo.

"Padre," she said, "today I'm sixty. Say something nice to me."

Padre Pio guarded a smile as he leaned toward her and whispered: "Death is near."

Some years ago a lady from St. Paul, Minnesota, told Padre Pio that her mother had been born near Pietrelcina, Padre Pio's birthplace. Padre Pio either misunderstood her, or he just acted waggishly, but he pretended to understand that the lady rather than her mother had been born in Pietrelcina. "Yes, I know," he laughed. "I heard you yell when you were born."

One day a group of about thirty men crowded into the single small office of the friary and nervously waited for Padre Pio. Their conversation indicated their anxiety: "Who will talk first? — What should I say? — What should we do? — Should I kiss his hand? — You introduce the group — No, *you* introduce us."

The moment of truth came. Padre Pio swung the door open and stood there, looking at them. Like the soldiers in the Garden of Gethsemane, they froze on the spot, spellbound, unable to move or say a word. With a broad, roguish smile, Padre Pio said: *"Buon appetito* — Good appetite." He closed the door on them and walked away.

When the door closed, the spell was broken. Bedlam broke out as they asked each other: "What happened? Why couldn't we move? Why didn't you say something? Why didn't *you* say something?"

Virgilio Volpe is a brilliant young singer and comedian in Italy. When he left his native America, he was offered an attractive career in the U.S. diplomatic corps. On Padre Pio's advice he chose the entertainment field instead. Virgilio asked Padre Pio whether he should keep his real name or adopt a stage name. With tongue in cheek, Padre Pio suggested: "How about taking the name Francesco Forgione!" Padre Pio had to reassure him: "I was only joking."

The humor of Padre Pio was not that of a TV comic. He did not play to the gallery. His humor was laced with wit, but it was always balanced with tact and charity. If someone had a bad day, Padre Pio would have a special little joke for him. He would listen to a visitor's conversation, but if the visitor had only small talk, after a few moments he would say: "Okay, stop!" He didn't have to explain that he was tired and in great pain, that his breathing was extremely difficult, and that he found his only consolation in praying the rosary.

After one Good Friday service, he showed how even his temperament was. The sacred liturgy had just commemorated the betrayal, suffering and death of Jesus on the Cross. At the end of the service, the participants were still in the sacristy. The atmosphere was solemn and serious. Everyone was silent. It was Padre Pio who broke the tension by chatting and joking almost with a spirit of levity.

Padre Pio's sense of humor was the salt of his ministry at San Giovanni. Certainly it can be used as one measure of his sanity. "The man suffered so much," one of his confreres said, "that if he had not had a sense of humor, he would have been manic-depressive."

It is hard to condense Padre Pio's ministry of fifty uninterrupted years into the few pages of a book. Even an amateur researcher could easily write a whole series of books on his prayer life, the prayer life which he fostered in his spiritual children, and his conspicuous social achievements.

In this chapter I will describe his daily routine. We will see Padre Pio at work inside and outside of the confessional, shepherding his sheep with an uncanny knowledge which led him to know their whole life story, even though he had never met them previously.

It is difficult to determine when Padre Pio's day began and when it ended. It began any time between midnight and 3:00 a.m. When he slept well, which was seldom, he slept a total of two or three hours. Most often, his nights were completely sleepless. When he did manage to sleep, his sleep was always fitful, never continuous. This almost total lack of sleep amazed the doctors. They could more easily explain a miracle than understand how Padre Pio could function without the refreshment of sleep.

"For Padre Pio," said Padre Eusebio, "sleep, if you can call it sleep, was a mixture of sighs and invocations:

'My Jesus, my Mother Mary, I offer up to you the groaning of my poor soul.' "

Until his death in 1954, Dr. William Sanguinetti was Padre Pio's personal physician. One day the doctor noticed how rough Padre Pio's bed was.

"I'm going to buy you a new bed," the doctor declared.

"Are you a rich man?" Padre Pio asked.

"No, I am not rich," the doctor said, "but at least I can buy you a new bed. Why do you ask if I am rich?"

Probably with tongue in cheek, Padre Pio replied: "Well, you know that Capuchins all live the same common life, and if you buy me a more comfortable bed, you will have to do the same for the 14,000 Capuchins in the whole Order."

The decision to buy one or 14,000 beds was not up to Padre Pio, but to Doctor Sanguinetti and Padre Pio's superior. Padre Pio alone got his new bed, and he used it because his superior told him to do so.

His 8 x 10-foot room, typical of the living quarters in the friary, served as his bedroom and study. On his desk were a small lamp, a picture of Mary, a picture of his parents, and a picture of the Pope. From his lightly upholstered chair he could see the picture of the Pope. He insisted that the shade of the lamp be adjusted to allow a ray of light to shine precisely on the picture. A prayer for the Pope began his day.

For many years Padre Pio offered Mass at 4:00 a.m. His confreres tried in vain to get him to schedule it at 4:30 or 5:00. Finally in his later years, he did change his time for Mass to 5:00 a.m.

After Mass and thanksgiving after Mass, Padre Pio had breakfast which consisted of coffee — one cup which he never finished. In his younger days, he didn't have that much for breakfast. When they urged him to take an egg, the suggestion always started a squabble.

It was in the confessional that Padre Pio wielded his

most powerful influence. He began hearing confessions shortly after Mass and continued until noon. His confessional for women was in the old church. The men confessed to him in the sacristy, kneeling down next to him. So many people went to confession to him that in January, 1950, the Capuchins began the custom of handing out numbered tickets. The average wait was ten days. When he was seventy-eight years old, he was still hearing confessions of fifty persons per day.

A lady from Solerno, now living in San Giovanni Rotondo, told me she had been going to confession to Padre Pio for twenty years. "I came in the beginning," she said, "because I had heard about this Capuchin priest with the stigmata of Jesus, and I simply kept coming, very, very often. It is only three-and-a-half hours from Solerno!"

As a rule, Padre Pio heard confessions only in Italian. If a priest or Bishop tried to confess in Latin, he brushed them aside with a brusque: "Go to another priest." Exceptions to this were singular.

He discouraged his fellow Capuchins from going to confession to him. "You have your own spiritual director," he told them. "Let me hear the confessions of these people. Don't take my time."

It made no difference what a person had to confess to Padre Pio. If the penitent wanted to make an honest confession, Padre Pio was like a lamb. Shopkeepers and doctors, priests and laity, North Americans, South Americans, Italians, Germans, Irish, and Australians, all told me the same thing almost as though their remarks had been rehearsed.

If a penitent were not honest before God, however, if he tried merely to go through the routine of reciting his sins without an honest intention to reform, Padre Pio was as merciless as was Jesus with the Pharisees. "Get out," he would growl.

He could read the penitent's soul. He knew if a person were disposed for absolution, or if he were merely curious. On a couple of occasions he told priests to get out of his confessional because they were dressed in sport clothes. Without a word of identification from them, he knew that they were priests. "Put on your habit, and then come back, and I'll hear your confession," he told them.

A young man in New York City, an absolute stranger to Padre Pio, told me that for a couple of years he had been carrying on an affair with his girl friend. Let's call him Charlie. Although he prided himself on being Catholic, he was unconcerned about reforming his life. His mother, on the other hand, was a very pious woman and devoted to Padre Pio. She wanted to confess to Padre Pio, and she asked Charlie to take her to Italy.

They arrived in San Giovanni Rotondo, and after a week their number came up for confession. Mamma's confession was uneventful, externally. Then Charlie tried to confess. Before he could open his mouth, Padre Pio barked at him: "Get out of here."

"I want to go to confession," he pleaded.

"I told you to get out," Padre Pio repeated more severely. Charlie was stunned, because he did not get the point of Padre Pio's censure. He left the confessional, but he was not easily discouraged.

He had heard that sometimes men confessed to Padre Pio in his room in the convento, and he asked the superior if he could do this. The superior agreed and indicated where he should wait for Padre Pio.

Padre Pio came along but passed by without a nod of recognition. Charles pursued the Capuchin, but Padre Pio entered his room and closed the door in his face.

Charlie posted himself at the door, determined not to let Padre Pio out of his room until he should hear his confession.

The door opened, and again Padre Pio snubbed him. "I came all the way from the United States to go to confession," Charlie protested as he followed Padre Pio down the corridor. "Why won't you hear my confession?"

Padre Pio whirled around, glowered at him, and said: "When you are willing to make a good confession, come back and I will listen to you."

For two years Padre Pio's words dogged Charlie's conscience. Finally they sank in, and he had his change of heart. He returned to San Giovanni Rotondo and waited in line for a week to confess to Padre Pio. Before Charlie could open his mouth, Padre Pio spoke to him, but this time the Padre was quieter than before. *"Finalmente!"* he said. "Finally! I have been waiting two years for you." Padre Pio heard his confession and absolved him.

A man who had grown up with Padre Pio as a child in Pietrelcina told me: "I couldn't fool that man. He could read your soul right down into your heart."

One day a doctor from Milan approached Padre Pio to go to confession. Padre Pio rebuffed him before he could begin. "Go away, you pig."

The doctor was furious. He denounced Padre Pio to his superior and demanded that he be censured. The superior knew that time would tell a different story. Two years later, the doctor returned, this time disposed for absolution. Padre Pio was, the doctor admitted, "like a lamb."

The doctor apologized to the superior: "Padre Pio tortured my conscience. He gave my conscience no rest." After his confession, the doctor became one of Padre Pio's staunchest supporters.

Outside of the confessional Padre Pio was not always "a lamb." One day the crowd at San Giovanni Rotondo was exceptionally large and boisterous. A priest and a Brother were trying to escort Padre Pio through the crowd as he sat in his wheelchair.

The Brother pushed and shoved and shouted, but they

could make no headway. Padre Pio began to shout: "Let me through!"

Slowly they began to move. "Don't let the Padre get upset," Padre Alessio was pleading.

When they finally got through the crowd, Padre Pio commented: "Don't worry. I don't get angry in my soul. I was shouting, but my heart was laughing."

His heart may not have been exactly laughing when the crowd milled around him. He was deathly afraid that some well-intentioned devotee might grab his hands to kiss them or to shake them. Also, fanatics often tried to cut off pieces of his habit.

On one occasion a visitor, in his exuberance, grasped Padre Pio's hand to kiss it. The Padre scowled angrily at him and pulled his hand away.

"What did I do?" the man asked, stunned. "What do you think!" Padre Pio answered him. "They are not decorations."

Afterwards he reassured his fellow Franciscans: "Don't worry. I don't get angry inside of myself. If I ever really get angry, it won't be because of people like him."

We have a conspicuous example of how Padre Pio dealt with people in the story of his encounter with Dr. Ezio Saltamerenda, the director of the Biotherapeutic Institute of Genoa. As a boy, Saltamerenda was stubborn. At nine, he lost his faith. At the age of fourteen he declared openly that he did not need God.

He read his Bible, but only to use it as a foundation for his atheism. He was the "compleat pagan." God does not exist, he convinced himself. God, if He exists at all, exists only for the weak and stupid.

One day on his way to Rome he stopped to visit a friend. His friend was a spiritual son of Padre Pio. A picture of the Capuchin stood on his desk. Suddenly a muscle spasm gripped Saltamerenda's throat. Unable to talk, he went home.

Later he went to Rome as he had originally planned.

But the next day he heard an interior voice, insisting that he return to San Giovanni Rotondo. He returned, and three times he experienced the same tightness in his throat.

Saltamerenda, as though in a trance, walked to the convento and waited for an hour-and-a-half for Padre Pio's return to the confessional. When Padre Pio returned, Saltamerenda only knelt and asked for a blessing for a sick relative. He had nothing more to say. He tried to stand but felt riveted to the floor.

Suddenly Padre Pio's voice jolted him back to reality: "Tell me, son, don't you ever think of your own miserable soul?"

"Certainly, Father," Saltamerenda answered, "or I couldn't go on living."

"And what is the purpose of living?"

Bewildered, Saltamerenda managed to answer: "For the propagation of the species."

"You wretch," Padre Pio snapped back at him. "Don't you see that your soul is being destroyed?" He placed his hand on Saltamerenda's mouth and said: "Go."

He left, but the touch of the priest's hand on his mouth had a profoundly disturbing effect on him. He felt compelled to return to Padre Pio. This time he hid among a group of men.

"Genoese," Padre Pio called out to him, "you have a dirty face. You live near the sea, but you don't know how to wash. You are a big ship without a captain."

More confused than ever, Saltamerenda tried to kneel down, but Padre Pio sent him away again. He wandered through the fields, feeling like a whipped dog. But he could not resist the hounding mental call of Padre Pio.

Again he returned to San Giovanni Rotondo. Padre Francesco brought him to Padre Pio's room. As they entered, the smell of violets invaded the corridor. "What do you want?" Padre Pio snapped. "Don't make me waste

my time. Go downstairs and I'll hear your confession."
The Genoese obeyed.

In the confessional Saltamerenda sobbed convulsively. As he began his confession, Padre Pio helped him by recalling all his sins, one by one, the sins of his whole life, secret sins and sins he had forgotten.

That evening, Saltamerenda was terrified by mysterious noises in his room. He heard loud knocking on the walls of his room and on the windows and doors. Mentally he asked Padre Pio's help, and the room became quiet, filled with Padre Pio's charismatic aroma.

Often penitents locked horns with Padre Pio in the confessional. They would lose, of course, to his uncompromising principles. Often they would later make a public confession, proud to identify Padre Pio as a miracle worker of God's grace.

One such person was Federico Abresch. "When I first went to see Padre Pio," he wrote, "I had recently converted from Lutheranism, but my conversion was purely for social reasons. I had no Faith. I was merely under the illusion of having Faith. . . . I was fascinated by the occult and the mysterious. A friend introduced me to spiritualism, but I soon grew weary of these inclusive messages beyond the tomb, and I threw myself eagerly into the field of occultism and magic.

"I met a man who declared that he possessed the only truth, theosophy. I became his disciple and accumulated books with most attractive and intriguing titles. With great self-assurance, I mouthed such words as reincarnation, logos, Brahma, and Maja, always awaiting that certain something both great and new that must surely come.

"I don't really know why, but I think that it was more to satisfy my wife that I still went to the Sacraments from time to time. I was in this state of mind when I first heard of that Capuchin Father, who, I was told, endured a living crucifixion and worked miracles.

"I was filled with curiosity . . . and decided to go and see with my own eyes.

"I went to confession to Padre Pio and he made me understand immediately that in my previous confessions I had omitted certain mortal sins. He asked me if I had been in good Faith. I answered that I considered confession a good institution, socially and educationally, but that I didn't believe at all in the divinity of the Sacrament. Then, deeply moved by what I had seen, I added: 'Now, Father, I do believe.'

"As if experiencing great pain, Padre Pio said: 'All the ideas you have had were heresies. All your Communions have been sacrilegious. You must make a general confession. Examine your conscience, and try to remember when you last made a sincere confession. Jesus has been more merciful to you than to Judas.'

"He glanced over my head and said in a loud voice: 'May Jesus and Mary be praised,' and he went into the church to hear the women's confessions.

"In the meantime, I remained in the sacristy, greatly moved and shaken. My head was spinning and I was unable to concentrate. I kept hearing those words again and again: 'Remember when you made your last sincere confession.'

"I hesitated, but I made the following decision. I would tell him that I had been a Protestant, that I had been rebaptized conditionally. Through that Sacrament, all the sins of my past life had been wiped out; but even so, for the sake of my peace of mind, I wished to review the whole of my past life from my childhood.

"When I returned to go to confession, the Father repeated the question: 'Well, when did you make your last good confession?' "I answered: 'Father, I happened to be . . .'

"At this point the Father interrupted me and said: 'Yes, you made a good confession when you were returning from your wedding trip. Leave out all the rest, and begin from there.'

"I was dumbfounded, overwhelmed by the realization that I had come in contact with the supernatural. The Father didn't give me time to think. He concealed his knowledge of my entire past under the form of questions. He enumerated with precision and clarity all of my faults, even mentioning the number of times I had missed Mass.

"After he specified all my mortal sins, he made me understand, with most impressive words, how serious my condition was. He added in a tone of voice which I can never forget: 'You have been singing a hymn to Satan, but Jesus in His tremendous love has broken His neck for you.' He then gave me a penance and absolved me.

"This absolution made me feel that I was suffocating. But later it caused me such joy and lightness that I returned to the village with the other pilgrims behaving like a noisy child.

"Humanly speaking, it was impossible for the Father to know that I had made a wedding trip and that the confession that I had made on my return was indeed a good one. It actually did happen just as he said. The day after we returned from the wedding trip, my wife said that she would like both of us to go to the Sacraments, and I complied with her wish. I went to confession to the same priest who brought me into the Catholic Church. He knew I was a novice, little accustomed to such things, and he helped me with questions. That is why I made a good confession.

"But now I ask myself: Who could have had any knowledge of these things, other than Padre Pio, who has the gift of reading our most intimate thoughts and can scrutinize our consciences?

"Only as a result of his gift could he have made me begin my confession from the time he chose, rather than from the time that I had in mind. From the beginning I was completely bowled over by hearing things that I had forgotten, and I was able to reconstruct the past by remembering in detail all the particulars that Padre Pio had described with such precision. Critics and doubters cannot say that this is a question of thought transference because, as I have already said, my intention was to begin my confession from my childhood."

Only if Padre Pio could not reach people in the privacy of the confessional would he bring his fist down on them in public.

One day a man visited San Giovanni Rotondo accompanied by his wife. His intention was to kill her. He had the whole scheme laid out for the return trip. He planned an "accident" for her car on the curving mountain road.

Padre Pio whirled around and pointed at him. "Murderer!" he roared out loud in public. "What are you doing here?" The man blushed and ran away, but he returned that afternoon to confess.

In a case less drastic but equally blunt, a man from Milan visited Padre Pio out of curiosity. He waited in the corridor between the friary and church until Padre Pio passed by.

"What do you want?" Padre Pio asked.

"I want to meet Padre Pio," the man answered, not recognizing him.

"You must go away, because you are dirty (*sporco*)," Padre Pio said. "I am Padre Pio and you are very dirty."

The visitor was highly indignant. "I have heard that Padre Pio is a saint," he said, "but I see that Padre Pio is a rude man."

"You must go away to prepare yourself to die," the Padre answered him, unmindful of his criticism. The man left, unreconciled. But the bold prophetic threat of death took on special meaning for him three months later when he detected a tumor on his throat. His doctor insisted on surgery. He returned to San Giovanni Rotondo, terrified and humble.

Padre Pio embraced him as a lifelong friend and encouraged him by saying: "You should not be operated on. The doctor must not touch you." The cancer did not become any better or any worse. After eight years the doctor was still expecting him to die at any moment.

"I got my miracle," the man boasted. "It was my conversion. Padre Pio gave me back my Faith."

At the opposite end of Italy, in Sicily, a railroad conductor interrupted his rounds on the train from Palermo to tell me how Padre Pio had brought his friend back to his Catholic Faith. His friend, Antonio, was a militant Communist in Milan. He saw nothing incompatible in calling himself a Catholic and a Communist. He had heard about the strange "monk" in San Giovanni Rotondo whose hands bled, so he and his conductor-friend decided to visit him.

They stood on the outskirts of the crowd which always surrounded Padre Pio. Suddenly Padre Pio shouted: "Antonio! Come here." Antonio, a perfect stranger to Padre Pio, approached him.

"How can you call yourself a Catholic and a Communist at the same time?" the Padre challenged him. "Take your pick. You are one or the other, but you can't be both."

This public revelation of his soul jolted Antonio into renouncing Communism and returning to the Catholic Faith.

One day, a mother and her five teen-age children visited Padre Pio. Rimini, their home town, is a sophisticated city, and the simplicity and poverty of San Giovanni Rotondo stood in sharp contrast to anything they had ever experienced. One of the girls, about nineteen years old, went to confession to Padre Pio. She was making her confession, when Padre Pio said to her: "*Cretina!* Stupid!"

She walked out of the confessional in a huff and told the people who were with her: "That is terrible. How can he do that to me? I will go back and tell him what I think of him!"

They pleaded with her not to go back to him but to go to another priest. "No, no," she insisted. "I'll go back to him and tell him what I think, because it is a terrible thing for him to say that to anybody."

She returned to the confessional and spoke her mind. The Padre answered her in a tender voice. "Oh," he said, "I thought you could take a joke."

Immediately she understood and calmed down. After Padre Pio gave her absolution, she went around to the front of the confessional and knelt down for his blessing.

Padre Pio looked at her, grinned, and said: "Your face shows that you are an intelligent person. Do you know what I'll do? I'll tell you three times: *Cretina, cretina, cretina!*"

This time she was thrilled to hear him say it. She realized that he was talking to her as a friend, and from then on she loved him dearly.

Usually, Padre Pio's abruptness was intentional. It served a purpose. A man from Pietrelcina, now living in Jamaica Estates, N.Y., told me: "Even if Padre Pio was rough, and I know a lot of people that this happened to, they appreciated the way he spoke. Even when he was rough, they found in their hearts that they had done something wrong. Then they were grateful to him, and they liked him all the more. Like myself. When he talked to me, I'd find out that something was not really the way I mentioned it. He told me the truth. I felt good. So the next time, I watched myself. He made you think. I found out a lot of things about myself."

Cleonice Morcaldi, a native of San Giovanni Rotondo and sister of the former mayor, told me: "So many people would come here for confession and Padre Pio would send them away. But he would torment them with remorse, and he would follow them with his prayers and his sufferings. Ultimately they would return, fully repentant. He never lost a soul which God had sent to him. He knew how to enter into the hearts of people. Many priests today absolve with: 'Very well, don't do it again,' and the same sins are committed again and again. But the real child of Padre Pio returned fully reformed. Padre Pio was another Jesus. He said to me: 'I know you inside and out, like you know yourself in a mirror.' That is why he minced no words. There was no halfway measure with him. But when it came to the poor and suffering, he had a love and a tenderness like Jesus.''

Padre Pio was most severe when penitents were not honest in making their confessions. Also, if people were merely curious, or going to confession to him only because it was the "thing to do," he would send them from his confessional, regardless of their status. "He threw Bishops out," his confreres told me, as if they could not believe what they themselves had witnessed.

Padre Angelico told me: "To Padre Pio, every person was equal. A camel driver was the same as a prince.''

One day Padre Angelico brought a married couple to Padre Pio for his blessing for themselves and their children. Three of their sons were in jail for burglary. Padre Pio almost attacked the parents. "I absolutely refuse to bless you!''

Padre Angelico persisted, but again Padre Pio refused. "You didn't pull in the reins when your children were growing up," he told the astonished parents, "so don't come along now when they are in jail and ask for my blessing.''

Some people thought that Padre Pio knew everything. Obviously, he was not omniscient. What he knew, he knew through his life in God. "Our Lord makes me remember," he explained, "only those things which He wants me to remember. Sometimes God introduces me to persons whom I have never met in my life, persons I have never heard of, for the sole reason that I should pray for them. In these cases, God always grants my requests. On the other hand, when the Lord does not want to grant my requests, He makes me forget to pray for them, although I had the best and firmest intention to do so."

Padre Pio did not always help people by giving them what they wanted, even though he knew that something tragic would happen. He wasn't a miracle worker by career, any more than Jesus was.

One day Padre Teofilo visited him to recommend to him a woman who had cancer. Padre Teofilo obviously was pressing him for a miracle. Padre Pio suddenly interrupted and said sharply: "Oh, stop it! You should rather think of your own life. It is hanging by a leaf of parsley." In less than two months, Padre Teofilo, the image of health, was dead.

Another time, Father Dionisio stopped in to say goodbye to Padre Pio. He was a newly ordained priest, on his way to Venice to continue his studies.

"Studies! Studies!" Padre Pio muttered. "Think of death, instead, so that when it comes . . ." His voice trailed off.

Padre Pellegrino, who was assisting Padre Pio at that time, complained to him: "What a way to say goodbye to Padre Dionisio!" Padre Pio didn't answer Padre Pellegrino. He only looked wistfully at him and shrugged his shoulders, as if to say: "There's nothing I can do." Twenty days later, the newly ordained priest was dead.

In the majority of cases, Padre Pio's knowledge of future events was a happy omen, or at least it shed a joyful ray of light on a somber scene. In January, 1936, three laymen were visiting him in his room. Suddenly Padre Pio knelt down and asked them to pray "for a soul soon to appear before the judgment seat of God." They all knelt down and prayed.

When they arose, Padre Pio asked: "Do you know for whom we prayed?"

"No," they answered. "We only prayed for your intention."

"It was for the King of England," Padre Pio said definitively.

One of the three visitors, Dr. Sanguinetti, remarked: "But Padre, just today I read in the paper that the King has only a slight case of the flu and that his condition is not serious."

"It is as I say," Padre Pio insisted.

About midnight, Padre Aurelio heard a knock on his door. There stood Padre Pio, who said: "Let us pray for the soul who at this moment is to appear before the judgment seat of God. It is the King of England."

The two Fathers prayed together for awhile. The following afternoon, newspapers told the story of the King's death precisely at the time Padre Pio had been in Padre Aurelio's room.

It was not unusual that people communicated with Padre Pio by mental telepathy (not to inject a more supernatural explanation at this point). For example, when a mother from Bologna and her five children visited him, she asked Padre Pio to accept them as his spiritual children. From that day on, for five years, she prayed every day: "Padre Pio, watch over my children. Protect and bless them."

Finally they had the chance to return to San Giovanni Rotondo. The mother begged him: "Padre Pio watch over my children. Protect and bless them."

Padre Pio answered her abruptly: "How many times are you going to ask me the same thing?"

"This is the first time I ever asked you," she said.

Padre Pio replied: "You have been asking me this every day now for over five years."

Sometimes it happened that Padre Pio's knowledge of the future also showed his subtle humor. Padre Angelico had been assisting at a shrine several miles from Alessandria, in northern Italy. A lady approached him and asked: "Are you Padre Angelico?"

"Yes, I am," he answered. "Why?"

"Padre Pio is waiting for you in San Giovanni Rotondo," she said.

Padre Angelico laughed off the incident as a case of fanaticism and delusion. There was no reason whatsoever for Padre Angelico to imagine any association with Padre Pio or with San Giovanni Rotondo. But within five months Padre Angelico received an order from Rome assigning him as economic administrator for the Foggia Province and for San Giovanni Rotondo.

Startled by this order from Rome and by the coincidence of the lady who first brought the news, Padre Angelico asked the authorities in the Vatican when the decision had been made to send him to southern Italy. He was told that the decision had been made only recently. Several months ago there had been no special need.

Padre Angelico arrived in San Giovanni Rotondo and met Padre Pio in the corridor. Padre Pio smiled at him and said: "You have finally arrived!"

Padre Pio's pre-knowledge of people and events sometimes disturbed people. A spiritual daughter now living in Rome told me of an occasion on which she became indignant until she was forced to admit that Padre Pio was right.

As she began to confess to Padre Pio, he interrupted her: "Don't speak. I'll tell you." Then he proceeded to enumerate her sins and imperfections. "You lied," he said, "and you allowed yourself to be distracted in church." Then he said, "You also got angry in church."

"He is out of his mind," she thought. "I never lost my temper in church." The Padre began to laugh, almost uproariously.

Startled by his laughter, and baffled by his reference to her anger in church, she tried to reconstruct what had happened. Then she recalled that the women in church were "jumping on him," as she described it, and "grabbing for his hands." She became angry as she saw the Padre grow pale with fear at the assault of those fanatical women.

"I'd like to take all of those women by the hair of their heads," she had said to herself, "and bang their heads together as if they were squashes."

When she heard Padre Pio laugh, she remembered how she had felt. Then the Padre added: "But you repented immediately." That little detail too puzzled her. "It was true," she told me. "I saw Padre Pio at the altar, and I saw him bless the people. I said to myself: 'If he doesn't get angry, why should I?' But could he know what I was thinking? How could he possibly know?"

Padre Pio did not always know. Nor would he make any pretense of knowing. Sometimes his only answer to a request for a favor was: "We must pray and wait for the will of God."

Padre Lino told me how his whole family had been gripped by misfortune in 1947. Padre Lino had just been ordained a priest, and after thirteen years of study he was preparing for his first Mass.

"I dreaded going home," he told me. "My sister was seriously sick with tuberculosis. My brother also was confined to bed. The whole family had been ill. Going home was like going to a hospital."

He visited Padre Pio and cried on his shoulder. "Don't worry," Padre Pio said. "Take courage. Your sister will be well. She is going to give you a party for your first Mass. Your brother, too, will be up and around. Just wait and see. Everything is going to be just fine."
Events followed exactly as Padre Pio had predicted.

After the party, Padre Lino returned to thank Padre Pio for his help.

"Tell your sister to throw away all the medicine." Padre Pio told him. "It's no good. Throw it away, all of it. Don't keep any of it." She did as directed and has enjoyed perfect health ever since.

About a decade later, Padre Lino's mother developed a malignant tumor. The doctor insisted on surgery. After Padre Lino asked Padre Pio's prayers, the doctor changed his mind about surgery. He substituted cobalt treatments. Immediately his mother began to improve. Again Padre Lino returned to thank his Spiritual Father. "You know," Padre Lino said, "those cobalt treatments are really helping my mother a great deal."

Padre Pio laughed and threw his arms up in the air in a gesture of frustration. *"Ecco cobalt! Ecco cobalt! Ecco cobalt!"* he grinned. ("Cobalt, he says!")

In San Giovanni Rotondo, a mother of a large family told me that she relied so heavily on Padre Pio's counsel that she called him her family doctor.

He never offered advice unless asked. When asked, he usually gave a direct answer. If people obeyed him, nothing would go wrong. If they disobeyed, a catastrophe would be sure to follow.

A certain young lady thought she had been having visions of Jesus. Padre Pio counseled her not to believe that the visions were genuine. She refused to let him guide her. She said that Padre Pio did not tell her the same things that Jesus told her in her visions. After a few months she committed suicide.

The head cook at the hospital, Laurino Costa, of whom we have spoken, was from northern Italy, not far from Padua. He had no desire to visit San Giovanni Rotondo, but he sent Padre Pio a telegram, asking his prayer that he find a job. Padre Pio telegrammed back to him: "Come to San Giovanni Rotondo at once."

Through an amazing series of coincidences, Laurino, penniless, arrived at about 4:00 a.m., in time for Padre Pio's Mass. After Mass, he followed a large group of men into the sacristy and stood toward the rear of the crowd.

Padre Pio, who had never seen Laurino before, beckoned to him to come near. Thinking that Padre Pio was gesturing to someone else, Laurino stood his ground. Padre Pio shouted at him: "Laurino, come, come here. I see you have arrived." Laurino approached him, trembling.

"Laurino, you will feed my sick," said Padre Pio, referring to the need for a cook in the Casa Sollievo.

"But Padre," Laurino argued, "I am not a cook. I've never even cooked an egg in my life. I don't know how to cook."

Padre Pio insisted: "Go and feed my sick. I'll always be near you."

Moved more by the insistence of Padre Pio's words than by his own free will, Laurino went over to the hospital and rang the doorbell. The Mother Superior welcomed him with the words, "You must be the experienced cook we have been waiting for."

Within three hours he started to work. He found everything strangely familiar. He not only did an excellent job of cooking, but he gave orders to the entire kitchen staff and dietitians as though he were a professional in hospital management. "To this day," he admits, "I still don't know what really happened. All day long I found myself calmly working and telling others what to do, as though I were carrying out a routine I had been used to."

When Laurino began cooking, there were about four hundred and fifty patients. Today he still cooks in the Casa Sollievo, now for over eight hundred patients and for the doctors and hospital employees as well. He claims that as soon as he leaves the kitchen, he is just as ignorant of any knowledge of cooking as he was fourteen years ago when Padre Pio tabbed him for the job.

Only when his health was poor did Padre Pio interrupt his routine and return to his room at about 10:00 a.m. Even then he didn't relax. He answered his mail and prayed his Breviary, the Divine Office.

He had the help of seven priests for the heavy volume

of the mail he received from all over the world — from the United States, Canada, and South America, from Italy, Ireland, England, Spain, Portugal, France, Germany, Poland, Yugoslavia and Czechoslavakia, from Egypt, Uganda, Kenya, Libya, New Zealand, Australia, India, Pakistan, Ceylon, the Solomon Islands and the Seychilles.

Father Dominic Meyer, his late secretary, said that in 1950 Padre Pio received about a dozen letters a week from England and Ireland. One day there were thirty letters from England alone.

By 1960, the volume of his mail rose to six hundred letters a day, plus fifty to eighty telegrams. About three-fourths of the letters were from Italy. Sometimes the number reached eight hundred a day.

From about 1965 onward, Padre Pio had lunch in his room at noon. The priests and Brothers would bring soup or *pasta,* vegetables, fish, or cheese and wine. Typical of the area, meat was seldom served. Regardless of what they served, the Capuchins had to insist that he eat something. He would hardly touch his food. He would nibble on it, and then push it away from himself. He would put his hands on this cinture and say: "Oh, I'm so full, I'm bursting."

His confreres argued with him: "But Padre, you didn't eat anything."

"He just laughed us off," said Padre Alessio. "If we ate the way he ate, we would not be able to live for a week."

The bigger the feast day, the less he would eat. Evenings, he would eat nothing. He would not even go to the refectory (dining room). He spent most of his time in his room, reading or studying or praying. He might have a glass of beer in his room, but he would only sip a small part of it and try to share the rest with anyone who might stop in for a visit.

During World War II, the American GIs, ever alert

to people's needs, heard that he liked beer, and they brought it to him by the case. In his later years, he gave up beer completely and drank water instead, flavored with a little sugar or lemon juice or anise.

After one of his blood tests, the doctors prescribed more protein in his diet, and peas were served to him. He ate a few spoonfuls, only to please the doctors. Yet he managed to sustain a constant weight of one hundred and sixty-five pounds on his five-foot eight-inch frame. Without food, he should have been weak and anemic. Except for his difficulty in walking, and a consumptive cough, he seemed to continue on as sturdy as a peasant farmer.

In 1948, Padre Pio had some stomach trouble. For eight days he had nothing except a little water. He had weighed himself shortly before his illness, and his superior told him to weigh himself after his eight-day fast. He had gained weight in the meantime! Padre Pio laughed heartily and commented: "I think I'll have to eat more to reduce!

Part of Padre Pio's afternoon was spent in his room, either in prayer or answering his mail. Part of his time was spent hearing the confessions of the men. For awhile he might sit in the shade of the tree just outside the friary door and chat with his friends. That is how he learned what was happening in the world. He never read newspapers or listened to the radio or watched television.

Sometimes he would stroll along the paths of the cloister garden behind the convento. The cloister is the area of the convento and grounds which no women are permitted to enter. There he would relax and chat with his confreres and male visitors.

Day after day, without a vacation or a day off, Padre Pio continued to shepherd his flock in the confessional and in his relaxed conversation with them. He made himself a prisoner of his people. Yet his vision was broad. He saw San Giovanni Rotondo as an integral part of the whole wide world and his interests were truly catholic.

As far back as 1921, he wrote to Bishop Poli, in Allahabad, India: "I have made the most insistent demands of my spiritual director to become one of your missionaries, but poor me, he didn't find me worthy. Up to now, there is no way I can possibly obtain this exceptional grace. . . . I will do my best to be a missionary in spirit."

The next year Padre Pio wrote to him again: "How much I desire, and how happy I would be, if I could find myself there in India so as to offer my poor work for the spread of the Faith. But if that good fortune is not reserved for me, but for other souls more noble and more dear to Jesus, I will exercise my mission with humble, fervent and efficacious prayer. Yes, Father, I remain here with my body, but in spirit I am near you and closely united to you."

This humility and obedience to his superiors were typical of his ministry in San Giovanni Rotondo. "I have worked," he wrote, "and I want to work. I have prayed and I want to pray. I have been attentive, and I want to be attentive. I have cried, and I want to cry always for my exiled brothers. I know and I understand that it is little, but this is what I know how to do. This is what I am able to do, and this is all that I can do."

Many times Padre Pio would stand at the window of his room or in the choir, puzzled by the throng of people in the piazza. "What are they doing here, all these people?" he would ask Padre Eusebio.

Padre Eusebio didn't know what to say. "I did not want to offend Padre Pio's humility," he said, "so I answered him: 'Padre, they have come to see me!' Then Padre Pio laughed to make me happy."

The crowds who came to visit him included not only the laity but Bishops and Cardinals too. Maria Pyle wrote that during the Second Vatican Council, between 1962 and 1965, "so many Bishops came to see Padre Pio that sometimes it seemed that the Council was at San Giovanni Rotondo.''

After the Vatican Council, the General Chapter of the Capuchin Order met in Rome. One of the Fathers from the General Chapter asked Padre Pio if he would care to send a message to Pope Paul VI. The Pope had recently issued his encyclical, *"Humanae Vitae,"* which emphasized the position of the Catholic Church on birth control.

For a full five years theologians had been clamoring for Pope Paul's own official policy statement on birth control. Then when he gave it, an uproar was heard from east to west. What a consolation it must have been for the Pope to receive this letter from the Wise Man of the Gargano:

> "Your Holiness:
>
> "Availing myself of your Holiness' meeting with the Fathers at the General Chapter, I unite myself in spirit with my Brothers, and in a spirit of Faith, love and obedience to the greatness of Him whom you represent on earth, I offer my respectful homage to your august person, humbly kneeling at your feet.
>
> "The Capuchin Order has always been among the first in their love, fidelity and reverence for the Holy See. I pray the Lord that its members remain ever thus, continuing their tradition of seriousness and religious asceticism, evangelical poverty, and faithful observance of the Rule and Constitutions, renewing themselves in vigorous living and deep interior spirit, always ready, at the least gesture from your Holiness, to go forward at once to assist the Church in her needs.
>
> "I know that your heart suffers much these days on account of the happenings in the Church: the absence of peace in the world, the

great needs of its peoples; but above all, the lack of obedience of some, even Catholics, to the lofty teachings which you, assisted by the Holy Spirit and in the name of God, have given us. I offer your Holiness my daily prayers and sufferings, the insignificant but sincere offering of the least of your sons, asking the Lord to comfort you with His grace to continue along the direct yet often burdensome way, in defense of those eternal truths which can never change with the times.

"In the name of my spiritual sons and of the 'Prayer Groups,' I thank your Holiness for the clear and decisive words you have spoken in the recent encyclical, *'Humanae Vitae,'* and I reaffirm my own Faith and my unconditional obedience to your inspired directives.

"May God grant truth to triumph, and may peace be given to His Church, tranquillity to the people of the earth, and health and prosperity to your Holiness, so that when these disturbing clouds pass over, the reign of God may triumph in all hearts, through the apostolic works of the supreme shepherd of all Christians.

"Prostrate at your feet, I beg you to bless me, my Brothers in religion, my spiritual sons, the 'Prayer Groups,' all the sick, that we may faithfully fulfill the good works done in the name of Jesus and under your protection.

"Your Holiness' most humble servant,

"PADRE PIO, Capuchin

"San Giovanni Rotondo, 12th September, 1968"

Padre Pio wrote that letter less than two weeks before he died. A confrere typed the letter for him. His own hands were unable to write a long letter. But there is no question that the ideas were Padre Pio's. Padre Clemente of Santa Maria in Punta handed it to the Vatican Secretary of State. It was published in *L'Osservatore Romano.*

During the General Chapter of the Capuchins, the Capuchin Father General had an audience with Pope Paul VI. With no special reason for mentioning Padre Pio, the Pope said: "Do all that you can to attract people who are not very well disposed to listen to the word of God. . . . Perhaps at first they will hiss at you. But I tell you that the same miracle will happen for you that happened for Padre Pio. Look at the fame he had! Devotees from all over the world flocked around him! Why? Maybe because he was a philosopher. Maybe because he was a scholar. Maybe because he had a way to help them. Maybe because he said Mass so humbly, heard confessions from morning to night. Maybe, and this is hard to put into words, because he was a marked representative of the stigmata of Our Lord!''

Seemingly stunned to hear this bold statement, the Father General could only add: "He was a man of prayer.''

The Pope agreed and said: "He was a man of prayer and suffering.''

Before Miss Mairead Doyle led a small pilgrimage from Ireland to San Giovanni Rotondo, her group visited Pope Paul VI. They mentioned that they were going to the tomb of Padre Pio. The Pope immediately commented: "Pray for me.'' Then he repeated: "Pray for me.''

The Pope let the ladies kiss his hand, and he blessed their religious articles. Then a third time he said: "Pray for me.''

Even before Pope Paul's election as Pope, when he was still a Cardinal in Milan, he sent a beautiful letter of congratulations to Padre Pio on the anniversary of his ordination to the priesthood.

When Padre Pio died, Pope Paul VI sent a telegram of condolence to "the whole population of San Giovanni

Rotondo," and he sent his personal representative to the funeral.

As far back as the pontificate of Benedict XV, the Popes knew of Padre Pio and they defended him. If only their advisers had shared their sentiments! On September 29, 1919, Pope Benedict XV sent a special blessing to him. The Pope wrote: "We hear that Padre Pio leads souls to God. As long as this mission of his goes on, we shall support him. Padre Pio is really a man of God. One must assume the duty of making him known. He is not appreciated as he deserves."

The same Pope told Bishop Damiani, of Uruguay: "Padre Pio is an extraordinary man indeed, one of those men on earth God sends from time to time to bring back all mankind to God."

CHAPTER 10

Spiritual Children

"I will station myself at the gates of Paradise. I will not enter until all my spiritual children have entered."

Padre Pio

In Padre Pio circles, the words "spiritual children" refer to two classes of people. First, they are the people who were under his wing in San Giovanni Rotondo. Also, they are people around the world who did not have the good fortune of meeting Padre Pio personally, but who placed themselves under his fatherly care. How he guided all his spiritual children and how he formed them as Christians should not be lost to history.

Murillo put two cherubs in his painting at the feet of Mary. If Murillo could return and paint the picture of Padre Pio, he would put three persons at his feet: Mary Pyle, and Padre Pio's own mother and father, Grazio and Giuseppa Forgione.

Mary McAlpin Pyle had been baptized "Adelia" as a child in the Presbyterian church in New York City. In 1918, six years before she met Padre Pio, she became a

147

Catholic. She was strongly influenced to embrace the Catholic Church by Maria Montessori, the internationally famed educator with whom she had toured Europe for ten years. Adelia began to use her "Catholic" name Mary when she became a Catholic. In Italy, she was called Maria.

From the time of her baptism, she searched for a spiritual director. Then on October 4, 1924, she visited San Giovanni Rotondo and met Padre Pio. Finally she had found the Wise Man who understood her and could guide her to God. She decided to build a home in San Giovanni Rotondo and to live permanently there. She made the move in 1925.

Her family took a dim view of her move because she exchanged her fine clothes for the plain, dull brown habit of the Third Order, the lay branch of the Franciscan Order which Saint Francis of Assisi founded for men and women.

Maria selected a site for her new home at a short distance from the convento. Padre Pio had advised her to buy a parcel of land higher up the hill and closer to the convento and church, but Maria had a mind of her own. She built her home down and around the slope that fell sharply away from the church. Every day she trudged up the rugged path for Mass and Holy Communion. Every Wednesday she went to confession to her Spiritual Father.

In the months before her death, Maria began to realize why Padre Pio had told her to locate her home closer to the top of the hill. Her illness confined her to bed, and she suffered mental torment at not being able to climb the hill and get to church and Mass. She considered this disappointment a penance for having disobeyed her spiritual director.

Maria left San Giovanni Rotondo only twice. During World War II she had to move to Pietrelcina for two years. The police had intended to put her in a concentration camp, but Padre Pio interceded for her and she was allowed to live with his parents in their home in Pietrelcina. In 1946, she returned to New York for a few months. Otherwise she never left San Giovanni Rotondo.

Most of Maria's time in San Giovanni Rotondo was spent working for Padre Pio. She was secretary for the heavy volume of his correspondence. Also, she was hostess to pilgrims who came to San Giovanni Rotondo to see him. She offered room and board to complete strangers. That they were friends of Padre Pio was enough of an introduction for Maria.

During World War II her home was a veritable U.S.O., for American and British servicemen. She fed them, quartered them, and arranged for them to see Padre Pio.

Maria used her family fortune well, not at all for herself, but for Padre Pio and the Capuchins. Through her, a friary and seminary were built in Pietrelcina, and she contributed generously to the construction of the church in that town. She purchased the house in which Padre Pio was born, and she contributed to the construction of Padre Pio's hospital.

But the disciple was not greater than the master. Like every Christian, she had to die to self that Christ might live in her. In 1931, many people accused Maria of being the culprit when Padre Pio was silenced by Rome. They said that she had told Alberto Del Fante about Padre Pio's miracles, and that it was the screaming headlines in the Italian newspapers which had led Rome to put Padre Pio into solitary confinement.

For the last two years of his confinement nobody spoke to Maria. When she approached the Communion rail in church, others would leave and let her receive by herself.

Her cat had kittens, and she wanted to share the news with her friends and neighbors, but no one would come near her.

In church, some ladies lit candles for the dead in her honor and recited prayers against the devil as their own private form of an exorcism.

When the restrictions on Padre Pio were lifted in 1933, the townsfolk forgot how they had treated her. When they went to her home to ask for charity, Maria never refused them.

Maria was not responsible for the uproar which Del Fante caused. Father Dominic Meyer, Padre Pio's secretary, called Maria "a discreet person." Padre Pio said of her: "She is a good religious, and the Lord knows how to give a just reward to those who have merited it."

Maria, had she been so inclined, had plenty of ways to sensationalize Padre Pio. She always avoided sensationalism. In a collection of twenty-two of Maria Pyle's letters which I was given, only one letter so much as mentions a miracle, and that miracle had already been widely publicized. It was a miracle not attributed to Padre Pio but to the Blessed Mother, when the Pilgrim Virgin's statue visited San Giovanni Rotondo and Padre Pio was cured of a serious illness.

Maria died in Padre Pio's hospital, as he had predicted, on April 26, 1968. She was eighty years old. The friars still remember her as their "mamma."

The two main guests whom Maria Pyle had in her home were Padre Pio's parents, Grazio and Giuseppa Forgione. With Maria, his own parents certainly rank as Padre Pio's dearest spiritual children. They lived and died in Maria's home.

Giuseppa's deep Catholic Faith absorbed her whole personality. If someone should say: "Tomorrow I'll do such and such a thing," Signora Forgione would bristle: "Who knows if you will still be alive or in the next world tomorrow? You should say: 'God willing, I will do it.' "

Whenever she visited Padre Pio, Giuseppa wore a snow-white blouse and kerchief. The people said she looked as if she had just come out of the laundry. Even in the middle of winter, she wore only thin clothing. Her friends offered her a coat, but she said: "I can't dress as a lady to see my son." She had to be herself, the same simple peasant woman who had raised Francesco and prayed and sacrificed for him to become a Capuchin priest.

Giuseppa abstained from meat on Wednesdays, Fridays and Saturdays, in honor of Our Lady of Mount Carmel.

Ten days before Giuseppa died, she paid her last visit to Padre Pio in the sacristy of the church. She stood before him, her arms straight down at her sides, her hands opened toward him. "How can we know before God," she whispered, "if we are not great sinners? We confess everything that we remember, but maybe God sees other things that we can't remember."

Her son consoled her by saying: "If we put all our good will into our confession and intend to confess everything, the mercy of God is so great that He will include and erase all that we can't remember."

Giuseppa had come to live with Mary Pyle in 1928. Her husband was to join her when he finished his work in the fields, but she suddenly developed pneumonia, and he came to San Giovanni Rotondo immediately. He was with her when she died on January 3, 1929.

Padre Pio stood at her bedside, but he didn't say a word. When she died, he leaned on her bed and cried profusely. Then he composed himself and said: "These are not tears of sorrow but of love."

For the next thirteen years Grazio continued to live in Maria Pyle's home. She gives us many insights into his simple but deep Faith. Maria tells us how Grazio tried to kiss his son's hand, but how Padre Pio told him that he had already told his mother that the son should kiss the hand of the parents, and not vice versa. Grazio complained, just as his wife had done: "I do not want to kiss the hand of my son, but I want to kiss the hand of the priest." Then Padre Pio would give him a bear hug, kiss him on both cheeks, and let him kiss his hand.

One day during Lent, Grazio came home and found a bottle of milk on the table. He regarded milk as a luxury. "What does this bottle mean?" he shouted. "Are you Christians or are you infidels? Don't you know that it is Lent?"

Maria and others in the house tried to remind him that some people in the house were sick and needed the milk. He rejected that emphatically. "Whoever is sick stays in bed, and whoever isn't in bed isn't sick and doesn't need milk."

Grazio was equally firm about not eating meat on Friday, even when the law might not oblige. "Jesus Christ Himself named this day Friday," he insisted. To Grazio, Friday meant "Don't eat meat."

His spirituality was almost cunning. On Good Friday, he told Maria Pyle very seriously: "Listen to the message which Padre Pio has sent. This is Good Friday, so everyone must eat on his knees, just like the Capuchins do at the friary. We must think of Our Lord Jesus Christ who died on the Cross for us."

After dinner, Dr. Puciano, who was present at the penitential meal, visited Padre Pio and thanked him for the penance of eating his Good Friday meal on his knees.

Padre Pio glanced over at his father. "I made them do it," his dad confessed sheepishly. But the Padre did not blame him. He smiled and said: "You did the right thing."

Slowly Grazio's health ebbed away. A short time before his death he attended Benediction of the Most Blessed Sacrament in his parish church of Saint Anne, proudly wearing the brown habit of the Third Order to which he belonged. His hair was as white as the cord which circled his waist. He remained on his knees for about three hours.

Grazio died in Maria Pyle's home, in his son's arms.

It was October 7, 1946, the Feast of Our Lady's Rosary. He was eighty-seven years old.

The international family which congregated in Maria Pyle's home was a reflection of a larger family which included Padre Pio and all his spiritual children in San Giovanni Rotondo. Some of his protegés were nationally and internationally famous.

"I was a Mason, I was an atheist," said Alberto Del Fante, a sheep whom he brought back to the fold. "I believed in nothing. Padre Pio has given me life in every way. Now I pray, now I attend Mass every Sunday. It gives me pleasure when my children, before they eat, make the Sign of the Cross and thank God who gave us our daily bread. Today I receive the Blessed Sacrament, and I am happy when God enters my body. Whoever has my courage will have my happiness."

When you ask Padre Pio's spiritual children to give you their impressions of him, their answers are almost identical. "He was God's gift," said Miss Margherita Hamilton, whom I met in Rome. "The first time I went to confession to him I started to weep — no, not to weep — it was as if I were ice and the ice was melting. This is the only impression I can give you, because water was falling out of my eyes. I am not a crying person. I never cry. I don't remember ever crying, even when my mother died. But when I first confessed to him, there were so many tears that I could scarcely speak."

Padre Pio fed his spiritual children the solid meat of the word of God in the most informal, familiar, relaxed, personal, palatable way.

A casual remark or favor, meaningless to anyone but the person concerned, would condition his children to follow his guidance. A word from him would lead them to pray the rosary, or to spend an hour in front of the Blessed Sacrament in church.

When his spiritual children followed his advice, often their financial or physical problems resolved themselves automatically. A young mother living in the Bronx, N.Y., wrote to me after she had started going to a psychiatrist: "I'll tell you that I honestly believe that this whole psychological experience is one of the mysterious workings of Padre Pio. I hated it at first, but at the moment I am so happy that it now has started and has taken the form that it has."

A nurse from Brooklyn, N.Y., wrote me: "Padre Pio helps me every day. I receive favor after favor. Apparently he is as concerned with people as always."

Alfonso D'Artega is a composer of international repute. He has directed symphony orchestras in the United States and Europe. His encounter with the Wise Man of San Giovanni Rotondo is typical of the way Padre Pio could jolt a person out of the ho-hum practice of his Faith.

"My wife and I allowed only two days," D'Artega told me, "when we visited Padre Pio for confession in 1964. I had to return to Rome in three days for a recording session. But Padre Vincenzo told us we would have to wait for five days. I was so depressed I almost cried. Four years I had waited to go to confession to Padre Pio. Now I had a ticket in my hand which gave me an appointment, but I couldn't use it. I didn't have the time to spare."

Feeling as though he had lost his best friend, D'Artega walked away from the office. Just then a man crossed the street and asked him: "Have you been to confession?"

"No," Alfonso answered, "I am very disappointed." D'Artega then explained how he had a ticket but that he couldn't wait for five days.

"I'll give you one," the man offered. "I've tried to give it to ten others, but no one wants it."

"I suspected he was making a deal with me," D'Artega told me, "so I asked him what strings were attached."

"Take it," the man told him.

He took it and returned to the convento. Padre Vincenzo was just closing the office, and D'Artega told him of his good fortune in obtaining a ticket.

"You can't take someone else's ticket," Padre Vincenzo warned him. But then he said in a whisper: "I don't see anyone. Maybe Padre Pio wants to see you."

"I asked when I could see Padre Pio," Alfonso continued. "I almost fell over when he said I could see him in one hour. An hour later I was in front of Padre Pio, shaking, trembling. But he was so sweet, so gentle. He gave me absolution right away, even with all my mistakes."

D'Artega returned frequently to San Giovanni Rotondo. He wanted to serve Mass. But he was told that was out of the question. "Everything here is previously arranged," he was told emphatically, "and we don't even know you."

Then one day, on a Wednesday, two minutes before Mass, a man came from the sacristy into the church and asked publicly: "Where is Alfonso Mexicano?" Everyone knew him as Alfonso the Spaniard, or the American, but nobody knew that he had been born in Mexico.

D'Artega looked up at him and said: "I am Alfonso."

The man, Giovanni Siena, told him: "Come on!"

In his excitement, D'Artega vaulted over the Communion rail and met Padre Pio as he was coming out of the sacristy. "I looked at him, and he looked at me," D'Artega said. "He seemed to say to me: 'I've been expecting you.' I served his Mass. Try to explain it if you can."

Afterwards, D'Artega spoke to Giovanni Siena and asked him how he had had the chance to serve Mass. Siena told him that for many years Gerardo De Carlo had served Mass every Wednesday without exception. But on that particular morning he had overslept.

Similar stories could be repeated by the hundreds, especially stories from World War II. Padre Pio assured his friends that San Giovanni Rotondo would not be bombed. It wasn't, although nearby Foggia was devastated. A spiritual son asked Padre Pio if his home town of Genoa would be bombed. He answered: "Genoa will be bombed." Then he grew pale, and his eyes filled with tears. "Oh, how they will bomb that poor city. So many homes, buildings, and churches will crumble."

Padre Pio turned to the man and smiled. "Be calm," he said. "Your home will not be touched." In the mass of ruins, the only house that remained standing in that area of the city was that man's.

When Padre Pio helped his spiritual children, he did more than extend a helping hand or tell them what would happen. The Wise Man of the Gargano used his gifts to lead his spiritual children not to the cult of himself, but to the love of Jesus Christ. He was indeed a Pied Piper, but he was also a priest, a good priest. His only thought was to decrease his own stature so that Jesus might increase. That talent, and not his miracles or bilocation, will probably go down as one proof of his being a saint. That may even be the reason why Jesus shared with Padre Pio the very marks of our Redemption.

Padre Pio began to shepherd his spiritual children to Jesus from the first contact he had with them. This he did in three steps. First, he would insist that they keep the commandments. Pietruccio, the blind man, told me that he once asked Padre Pio what he had to do to be saved.

Padre Pio answered: "It is enough if you keep the commandments of God and of the Church. That is enough to save your soul."

From that point on, if his spiritual children were still running with him, Padre Pio would hand them the two-edged sword of prayer and meditation.

I asked many people if Padre Pio had any rules or methods for prayer. Nobody knew of any. On the other hand, he did have some guidelines for them. He didn't let them identify prayer with "turning everything off" as in yoga.

"Pray with your heart and with your mind," he told Pietruccio. "It is useless to pray only with the heart, without the mind. If we pray without paying attention to what we are saying, we will have the curse of the Lord, not His blessing. So when you pray, be very careful to pray with your heart and your mind, with *all* your soul."

As a help in praying with *all* their souls, Padre Pio insisted that his spiritual children go to Mass and Holy Communion every day. Also that they pray the rosary daily. These were to be their basic prayers.

Prayer was to be their first input into the spiritual life. Then, as they began to advance in the love of God, he led them to take the third step on their way to perfection. He counseled them to spend a half hour in meditation, reflecting on the truths of our Faith, especially on the Real Presence of Jesus in the Blessed Sacrament. He told his spiritual children that if they would pray for half an hour, they would soon see they needed more than a half hour for meditation.

It seems that Padre Pio attached considerable importance to the use of a book for meditation. "You can meditate on any of the truths of our Faith," he said. "By using a book, you can help your mind to single out a specific, graphic topic for meditation."

One day Pietruccio complained to Padre Pio: "I can't pray very attentively." Padre Pio answered him: "In that case, go near to Our Lord in the church anyway, without saying anything or doing anything. It is enough if you give Our Lord your time. Our Lord is happy at least to receive us because of the time we give Him."

When Padre Pio was the spiritual director of the boys in the seminary in San Giovanni Rotondo, one of his fledglings was having a hard time keeping his mind on the theme of the meditation. The boy struggled to ward off distractions. At the end of the meditation, Padre Pio came up to him and patted him on the back. *"Bravo,"* he said.

In 1919, Padre Pio wrote a letter to one of his spiritual daughters, who apparently thought she was not getting anywhere in prayer because she did not feel the presence of God. "If I am not mistaken," he wrote to her, "the real reason you don't experience the presence of God, or rather you don't succeed in making your meditation well, is that you do the following: you approach the meditation with a kind of arrogance, with a great anxiety to find some subject that will please and console your spirit.

"This is enough for you never to find what you are looking for. Your mind does not deal with the truth which you are meditating on, and your heart is empty of affection. My daughter, when someone is looking for something anxiously and hurriedly, he will touch it a hundred times without noticing it.

"By useless anxiety, you will only become spiritually very tired, and your mind will not be able to rest on the subject which you are considering. For this reason your soul itself is responsible for becoming cold and stupid.

"The only remedy I know of is this: get rid of this anxiety, because it is one of the worst traitors to real virtue which devotion can have. It pretends to warm us up for good works, but it doesn't. Rather, it chills us, and only makes us run in order to stumble. So you must, as I have often told you, always be careful, especially in prayer. To succeed better, remember that grace and the taste of prayer are not drawn from earth but heaven.

"It is necessary that we use the greatest care and every effort to dispose ourselves, but always humbly and calmly. Even if we should use all our strength, we are not the ones who pray and draw down grace by our own efforts. It is necessary that we hold our hearts open to heaven and wait for the heavenly dew to descend. Don't forget this, my daughter. How many courtiers come and go in the presence of the king, unable to speak to him or hear him? They are only seen by him. In this way, we show ourselves as the king's true servants. This is the way to be in the presence of God, just by declaring with our will that we want to be His servants. This is a holy and excellent way, pure and perfect.

"You may laugh, but I am speaking seriously.

"We put ourselves in the presence of God to speak to Him and to hear His voice by means of His internal inspiration and illumination. Usually this gives us great pleasure, because it is a significant grace for us to speak to so great a Lord. When He replies, thousands of perfumes descend on the soul and cause great joy.

"If you can speak to Our Lord, praise Him, listen to Him. If you cannot speak because you are uncouth, don't be unhappy. Shut yourself up in a room, and, like a courtier, pay Him homage. He who sees you will be glad for your patience. He will prefer your silence.

"On some other occasion He will prefer to console you. Then He will take you by the hand, speak to you, and walk a hundred miles with you along the paths of His garden of prayer. Even if that never happens, which is really impossible, because the Father cannot bear to see His creatures in perpetual turmoil, be content all the same. Our obligation is to follow Him. Consider it a great honor and grace that He should take us into His presence.

"In this way, don't bother yourself about speaking to Him. The other way, just standing by His side, is no less useful. Perhaps it is even better, although less to our taste. So when you find yourself with God in prayer, reflect on the truth, speak to Him if you can. If you cannot, remain there. Make yourself seen, and don't make yourself a nuisance."

The pen of Padre Pio which gave us these magnificent thoughts dried up in 1922, when the Vatican forbade him to write any more letters. What a treasury of his guidance those letters would have been had he been able to continue writing like that until his death in 1968!

Fortunately, we have another letter to a spiritual daughter which analyzes the stages of the spiritual life. His guidance is not academic when he writes:

"Remember that the love of God is continuously growing in the soul. You can watch it. You will always feel ready for anything in the service and honor of God, even though your soul will not feel an attraction and your spirit will be completely empty of any feeling. On the contrary, you will feel surrounded by darkness, and everything you do will be done with great difficulty and repugnance.

"After all this, I don't know if the purge will end. It seems to me that there is another grade of contemplation to which Our Lord invites us. If it is true, and I hope and am firmly convinced that the Divine Doctor will lift you still higher, then I'll not add another word, except to urge you to be faithful and humble. Keep the great Mother of God before your mind. The more she was exalted, the more she humbled herself.

"I'll warn you that at this point, dryness alone is not sufficient for the purging of the soul. There is need of another interior cause of pain, which penetrates the whole soul, piercing it intimately and renewing it completely.

"This light transfixes the soul in its sins and upsets the poor soul as if to put it into a state of extreme affliction, with interior pains of death. Yet, in this light, which at first surrounds the soul with such abandonment and pain, there is something which eventually transforms the soul and lifts it up into mystical union.

"How that happens, I don't understand. Only I tell you without fear of making a mistake, or of telling you a lie, that it will happen this way, and not in any other way. The soul will experience atrocious pains, as if penetrating the sufferings of the damned in hell. The light which is the cause of this horrible suffering will render the soul capable of receiving the kiss of perfect union of love and clothe it with a brilliant light.''

By praying with one's whole mind and heart, Padre Pio didn't mean *feeling* the presence of God. "You are mistaken right from the beginning," he wrote to a spiritual daughter, "if you think that God doesn't love you any more just because you don't feel His love in your will or in your heart, or because you don't experience any sweetness in your love of Him.

"That is painful, and I understand this state of your soul very well. All of this is necessary when a soul is being called by God to a high form of perfection. It is with good reason that I say this. This is a painful period for the soul, because the poor creature is forcing itself to serve and please God in everything, and this is from its own point of view. There is nothing wrong in the way it is working for God, if in all its devotions the will is parched and the heart is without any feeling for supernatural things.

"What is worse, very often the soul feels itself horribly divided. The lower appetite finds itself afflicted with troubles, with dryness and with pain.

"But don't let us be frightened when we are confronted with this state. Lucky soul! Even when the soul is plunged into this dense darkness, it can still receive a little light so as not to fall into despair.

"When God sees that the soul has become strong in His love, affectionately united to Him, and already withdrawn from earthly things and from the occasion of sin, and has acquired sufficient virtues to stay in His service without all these attractions and tangible sweetness, then He takes away the sweetness of the affections which until that time have been felt in all devotions and meditations.

"What is more painful for the soul, He takes away the power to pray and to meditate, and He leaves the soul in the dark, in complete and painful dryness.

"In the face of such a change, the soul is at first terrified. A person might think that this fear is due to some mortal sin into which he has fallen. He is afraid of being in disgrace before God. What a mistake! What the soul thinks is abandonment is nothing other than exceptional grace of the heavenly Father. This is the transition to the capacity for contemplation. It is dry at the start, but afterwards, if a person perseveres, the soul will be lifted from meditation to contemplation, and everything becomes sweet and pleasant.

"The soul is then preoccupied with a sense of love, and that is the reason for its pain. But the poor soul can't become comforted. It thinks that nobody knows the real condition. If only the soul could realize that the impossibility of centering the imagination on a point of meditation is due to God. He subtracts from the imagination that bright light which had previously helped it work on supernatural things.

"Now God infuses a better light into the intellect, a much more spiritual light, a purer one which enables the soul to fix the mind on God and on divine things without any discursive reasoning. Now the soul can contemplate God with a simple vision, ever so sweet, delicate and divine."

Apart from the Mass and confession, the main suggestion Padre Pio offered his spiritual children for a prayer-life was devotion to the Blessed Virgin Mary. "*Mammina*," he called her, "my dear little Mother." He gently but ever so firmly thrust devotion to her upon all his spiritual children. He said: "I'd like to have a voice strong enough to invite the sinners of the whole world to love Our Lady."

The form which Padre Pio's devotion to Mary took was the rosary. He never let it out of his hands. One of the Brothers told me: "I'm surprised that the rosary didn't grow root right in his fingers."

Just two days before he died, Padre Pio told one of his spiritual daughters: "Love the Madonna. See to it she is loved, and recite her rosary. It is the weapon against the evils of the world today."

When asked how many rosaries he recited, he replied: "I'm satisfied only when I have said my sixty rosaries."

Amazed by his answer his friend asked him: "But Padre Pio, how can you pray that much?"

He answered: "How can you not pray that much?"

One day Padre Eusebio visited Padre Pio in his room, quite proud that he had recited three rosaries of five decades. "I thought I had prayed enough to earn a word of praise from him," Padre Eusebio said. "I asked Padre Pio how many rosaries he had said — forty? I was thinking of what he had said a few days previously."

Padre Pio answered him: "More than I told you."

"More than forty?" Padre Eusebio questioned him.

"I have said sixty rosaries of fifteen decades. But keep it to yourself."

We might wonder how that was physically possible. But if we realize that he never wasted a moment, that he was always fingering his rosary even when people milled around him, and if we recall that he hardly ever slept, we might begin to understand how Padre Pio's *spirit* of prayer could lead him to say that many rosaries.

One day Padre Pio attended a play at the hospital which depicted the martyrdom of Saints Peter and Paul. He had been anxious to attend the play, and he watched it intently. But all the while he held his hand on his breast pocket, constantly praying the rosary.

Father Daniel Hickey, who visited Padre Pio over sixty times, wrote under oath: "Padre Pio was usually seen standing with his right hand in the front-fold breast pocket of his Capuchin habit. A few times when he withdrew his hand, he was seen to be fingering a small chaplet of beads. Someone told me later that the prayers of the chaplet were all short ejaculations which could be said easily in a second or two, almost as fast as a person could leisurely finger the beads themselves. It seems it was Padre Pio's habit not to waste a second but to fill each one with prayer. At any lull in the conversation, no matter how short, his lips would be seen to move slightly as he prayed a few more of the short prayers. But there was nothing ostentatious in all this; it was a long time before I was aware of what he was doing, though I had noticed his hand constantly in the breast pocket of his habit."

It was Mary of whom Padre Pio was thinking when he felt a fire burning in his heart. He said that the fire was so hot that he "felt the need to put ice on it to extinguish it and to keep it from burning me up."

Mary was so familiar with him that when she appeared to him, her appearances did not startle him. He thought everybody saw her. "With what care Mary accompanied me to the altar this morning," he wrote to his spiritual director. "It seems to me as though she had nothing more to do than to think about me."

On August 5, 1959, Padre Pio received a singular favor from Mary. By a special concession of the Pope, the Pilgrim Virgin, a statue of Our Lady of Fatima, was brought by helicopter to San Giovanni Rotondo. For three months Padre Pio had been confined to bed, seriously ill. Against the wishes of the doctor, he insisted on getting up. With the permission of his superior, and supported by two strong Capuchins, he half-walked and was half-carried from his room to the church where the statue was venerated.

Three times he had to stop. Finally he made it to the church.

"Dissolved in tears from pain and fever," a writer described, "he knelt before his Queen in prayer and reverently kissed the base of the famous image of Our Lady."

He had only enough strength to return to his room and to his bed. At 2:15 p.m., the helicopter took off, carrying the statue to other cities of Italy. It made three passes over the piazza and convento, directly opposite Padre Pio's window. He could see the statue of Mary through the helicopter window.

"*Madonna mia,*" he moaned. "The day you arrived in Italy I became sick. Now you are leaving, and you leave me like this . . ."

The pilot, as he pulled away, felt a sudden impulse to swing back toward the convento. Padre Pio himself tells us what then happened: "At that moment I felt a shudder in my bones, and I was cured immediately." He got out of bed and went about his work as though he had been healthy all his life. Later he wrote the account of his cure in a letter to his superiors in Rome.

Besides devotion to our Blessed Mother, Padre Pio had strong devotion to St. Francis. We have already mentioned his devotion to his Guardian Angel. Also he had devotion to St. Dominic and St. Catherine of Siena, because of their devotion to Our Lady of the Rosary.

All during his life he had devotion to St. Joseph. He prayed to him every day. But for two or three months before Padre Pio died, he did something unusual. He said he would like to have a picture of St. Joseph, and he asked his confreres to put it on the veranda. Every day on his way to bless the crowds from the choir window, he stopped momentarily in front of the picture and prayed. "We never realized at the time," a Brother told me, "that he was praying to St. Joseph, the Patron of a Happy Death."

Padre Pio had these devotions, but he never urged any of them on his spiritual children except his devotions to Mary and to the Poor Souls in Purgatory.

"More souls of the dead," he said, "come up that road in front of the friary than souls of the living." His encounters with them sound fantastic. But we have more than his word that he met and dealt with visitors from Purgatory.

Padre Raffaele, who was Padre Pio's confrere in San Giovanni Rotondo for thirty years, told me two stories about Padre Pio and the Poor Souls. One day Padre Pio was alone in the choir in prayer when he heard a noise in the church. He went to investigate and discovered that the large candles at the base of the statue of Mary had been shattered and were lying on the floor. The statue was so high that nobody could have reached the candles without a ladder. Padre Pio turned around and saw a Capuchin Brother kneeling there.

"Who are you?" Padre Pio called out.

The Brother answered: "I am a Capuchin novice from Purgatory, and I am here doing penance for my sin, the lack of diligence. . . ."

"Well," said Padre Pio, "this is a fine way to do reparation for your sins, by smashing up all those candles. Go away now. Tomorrow I will say a Mass for you. That way you will be freed, and you won't have to come back here."

The novice thanked him and left. Padre Pio then realized that he had been talking to a dead novice, and a cold shiver ran up his spine. He hurried out of the church and found Padre Emmanuele and told him what had happened. They returned to the church and found the broken candles, just as Padre Pio had described.

The other incident of which Padre Raffaele spoke also involved a visit of a soul from Purgatory. On a cold November day in 1918, Padre Paolino's sister visited the friary. After supper, Padre Pio joined them in the guest room. Padre Paolino suggested that he and his sister pay a visit to the Blessed Sacrament. Padre Pio remained by the warmth of the fireplace.

Before long, Padre Pio fell asleep. Suddenly he woke up. He was startled to see an old man bundled up in an overcoat, warming his hands at the fire.

Padre Pio asked him who he was and what he was doing there.

"I am from Purgatory," the man said, "and I am doing penance." Padre Pio promised to offer a Mass for him in the morning and escorted the man out of the friary as far as the tree in the piazza.

Returning to the friary alone, Padre Pio tried to get in. But the door was locked and bolted from the inside. He rang the bell and Padre Paolino opened the door. He asked Padre Pio how he had gotten outside. Padre Pio said the door had not been locked. But Padre Paolino insisted that it had been locked. We are left to draw our own conclusion to this incident.

Padre Pio's love for the Poor Souls in Purgatory was all-consuming. "Pray, pray, pray," he told his spiritual children. "We must empty Purgatory. All the souls in Purgatory must be liberated."

When the Church took away some indulgences, Padre Pio was dumbfounded. "Now," he said, "who will think of the Holy Souls? Pray for them a great deal."

It seems clear that certain people who had died were allowed to go to Padre Pio and request favors for their families. Often he would assure his friends that the people they asked about were in heaven, or that they might still be in Purgatory. Someone who never met Padre Pio personally might be inclined to snicker at such a revelation. But those who knew him realized that he did not speak lightly of these matters. His whole life and personality gave them unquestionable proof that he knew what he was talking about.

We can count in the millions the number of Padre Pio's spiritual children who loved him dearly. Their letters attest to this. The friars saved all their letters and built a storeroom as large as a garage next to the friary. The storeroom eventually became full, literally packed with an estimated two million letters from all over the world, thanking Padre Pio for favors small and large. In 1968, a visitator from Rome ordered the Capuchins to destroy all those letters. The Capuchins obeyed.

The loss is irreparable. But there is no real consternation among the friars. First of all, it was an order under obedience, and Capuchins are vowed to obey legitimate authority. They saw the value of their vow of obedience in the life of the Wise Man with whom they lived. But the volume of letters on file is quickly being restored by Padre Pio's spiritual sons and daughters, who write to San Giovanni and tell the Capuchins how they still experience the power of Padre Pio's prayers and feel his presence.

When people wrote to Padre Pio before his death, asking him to accept them as his spiritual children, he asked only that they live a Christian life by keeping the commandments of God and the Church.

Now that Padre Pio is in heaven, we can be sure that he will accept any and every person on the same terms. People who ask that favor of him are amazed at the protection they receive, and especially at the peace and joy which they experience in their souls. There is no harm in everybody putting Padre Pio to that test!

Not only did people visit and write to San Giovanni Rotondo. About a hundred and fifty people or families from around the world have felt so strongly attracted to Padre Pio that they have moved, lock, stock and barrel to San Giovanni Rotondo.

"I feel it my duty to remain here," a young lady from Uruguay told me. "I'll never leave this town even for a visit home."

"For me," she said, "Padre Pio was everything. I talk with him all day in my imagination. I need this. He is everything. Maybe things would be the same if I should live elsewhere. But I think that there is something special here, near his tomb, near his body. I feel it is my duty to remain here. He led me here, and I am supposed to stay here. Through him I have been saved. He is my patron. He has offered his own blood for me, so he is the boss. I need him as a father and mother, because of his tenderness.''

When I visited San Giovanni Rotondo in 1971, signs were displayed all over the town: *"Viva Padre Pio!"* You can translate that: "Long live Padre Pio!" But considering the magnetism which that man of God still exerts today over his spiritual children, you may well translate the signs: "PADRE PIO LIVES!"

CHAPTER 11

Phenomena

As I was preparing for Mass one day in the crypt in San Giovanni Rotondo, a young Spanish-speaking mother interrupted me. She had just arrived from Guayaquil, Ecuador, and I was the first priest she met. Thinking that I was assigned to the friary, she blurted out her story. Her son had been killed in an automobile accident and Padre Pio brought him back to life. She had a full dossier of proofs from her doctors and parish priest.

At the time she spoke to me, I was preparing to offer Mass for a group from Ireland. The group's tight travel schedule prevented me from talking to the lady at length. I directed her upstairs to the friar on duty who could introduce her to Padre Lino, to whom she should tell her story.

Immediately after Mass I hurried upstairs to learn all the details of her story. Imagine my shock and disappointment when I could not locate a single person who could remember having spoken to her. Overreaction to an alleged miracle, I thought, would be one extreme, but indifference to documentary evidence was incomprehensible. There is no sequel, and there can never be a sequel, to that story.

The next day I met a priest, his mother, his sister and his brother, all from Vienna, Austria. The priest told me that his brother had survived an "impossible" kidney operation and had driven 450 miles to thank Padre Pio.

Accounts such as these have been and still are almost daily occurrences in San Giovanni Rotondo. The Capuchins there might jot down a reference to the more spectacular reports, but even when they do, it is hard to detect even a ripple of excitement or emotion.

Nor do they save letters unless they are considered important. As an example of an *unimportant* letter, I quote verbatim from a letter which was received from Mozambique while I was in San Giovanni Rotondo:

"Dear Father Lino, some people have asked me to mention to you the graces that they have received. A small girl who had worms in her stomach for two years could not be cured by doctors, so her mother prayed to Padre Pio, and now she is completely cured.

"A young boy was very ill. His father is a doctor, and he couldn't find out what the boy had except by operating. So his granny prayed for help to Padre Pio, and after touching him with the rosary, it wasn't necessary to operate.

"Also, another person who was supposed to be operated on, prayed to Padre Pio to cure him. Soon after he was cured without being operated on."

The Capuchins were happy to receive the letter, but they read it, and that's all there was to it. Every day they receive about seventy letters from English-speaking countries alone, which relate favor after favor attributed to Padre Pio. But scant attention is paid to most of them.

A host of people living in San Giovanni Rotondo, perhaps the majority, have received special favors, large and small, from the beloved Padre. But it was extremely difficult for me to obtain their stories. I was a priest, and the people wanted me to tell them how to pray the rosary more devoutly or how to be more recollected in their half-hour thanksgiving after Holy Communion. That's the way Padre Pio had spoken to them, and that's the way they expected a priest to speak to them now. They saw no need to converse with a priest about their miracles.

Priests and laity alike in San Giovanni Rotondo realize that miracles did not make Padre Pio holy, nor do miracles make people who receive them holy. What makes a person holy is love for Jesus Christ.

If a miracle is claimed, maybe it will be investigated, maybe it will not. In any case, the final judgment of facts rests with the Vatican. In the canonization process now going on for Padre Pio, no miracle will be investigated unless it happened after his death. That is the typical procedure of Rome. We will have more to say about the canonization process.

In this chapter, I will present highlights of the interviews which I had with some of Padre Pio's spiritual children. In doing this, I do not claim to have any final voice in stating that the alleged miracles are authentic. The Church will make that determination, if and when she decides to investigate them.

However, I have solid reason to believe that events narrated by the persons in this chapter are true. The parties themselves are reliable. Also, other people have vouched for their authenticity. And finally, objective facts often corroborate their word.

Each of these stories is a "first person" story, told directly to me in a personal interview with the parties named.

INTERVIEW WITH GIOVANNI SAVINO
San Giovanni Rotondo, Italy
July 17, 1971

It was 2:00 o'clock in the afternoon on February 15,

1949. We had placed a charge of dynamite under a tremendous boulder during the construction of a one-room addition to the convento.

At 12:00 noon, another member of the Third Order of St. Francis and I set the charge and lit the fuse. We waited one minute. There was no detonation. We waited again, but still the charge didn't go off. I went over to take a look, when suddenly the dynamite exploded in my face. Everything, even the boulder I was standing on, flew into the air. The boulder cut off a branch from a tree. The boulder would have split me into two pieces if it had hit me.

A shower of rock hit me in the face. The rock that I had been standing on fell on me. I lost consciousness. My face was all burned. All the skin of my face was torn off. Padre Raffaele came over and gave me first aid. Padre Pio heard about the accident and asked Brother John to get Dr. Sanguinetti. The doctor saw that my right eye had been blown out of its socket. My right eye was gone entirely. The socket was completely empty.

They took me to Foggia and left me in the hospital. Then the words which Padre Pio spoke three days before the accident began to make sense. Every day after Mass, and before going to work, I had knelt down by the stairway at the end of the corridor and said: "Padre Pio, give me your blessing. I am going to work." He put his hands on my head and blessed me.

On the third day before the accident, on the morning of February 12, Padre Pio threw his arms around me and embraced me.

"Courage," he said, "I'll pray to the Lord that it may not cause your death." He then walked away and went upstairs. I didn't know what he was talking about.

The same thing happened again the following morning, on the thirteenth, fourteenth, and fifteenth. I asked him for his blessing, and each time Padre Pio said the same thing.

On February 15, Padre Raffaele passed by. I said to him: "Something is going to go wrong for me today, because Padre Pio told me so."

I didn't let his words bother me. I returned to work, indifferent to what I heard, because only God knows what is going to happen. And Padre Pio knew it too. Maybe the accident could not be avoided. Maybe things had to happen that way.

After the explosion, they took me to Foggia. For three days I was in shock. My whole head and face were bandaged. There was not much hope of saving my left eye. They thought they could save it by an operation. They said that there was nothing they could do for my right eye. It was completely gone.

After three days, I heard the doctor enter my room. I told him: "Doctor, I don't want to make Padre Pio seem strange, but I smelled his tobacco as I lay in bed. I was saying to Padre Pio: 'Send me a little tobacco,' and I smelled his aroma."

A week later, ten days after I entered the hospital, I woke up at 12:30 or 1:00 o'clock in the morning. I could hear the breathing of the two or three men sleeping next to me. I felt someone give me a light slap on the right side of my face, the right side where the eye was completely gone.

I asked: "Who touched me?" There was nobody. Again I smelled the aroma of Padre Pio. It was beautiful.

In the morning they brought me to an oculist for treatment. He unbandaged my face and head. I had all new skin on my face. I told the doctor: "I can see you!"

He told me: "Turn to the right so you can see me with your left eye."

"No," I told him, "I see you with my right eye. I don't see anything out of my left eye."

"Are you crazy?" he said. "I am telling you that your right eye isn't there any more. I'm treating only your left eye."

"Doctor," I told him, "I am not crazy." I wanted to tell him: "Maybe you are crazy. The right eye is the one I see out of, not the left." He was an atheist and didn't believe anything. He didn't understand anything.

He covered my left eye and asked me: "How many fingers am I holding up?"

"Five," I answered. "That's how many!"

He was astonished. He asked: "Who is your protector?"

I told him: "Padre Pio."

He looked at me and saw that my right eye was in its socket. He could see it. He said: "Now I believe, too, because of what my own hands have touched."

That summer Padre Raffaele wanted to send me to another oculist, at the Polyclinic Hospital in Rome. I went to Padre Pio and said to him: "Padre Raffaele is sending me to Rome. He says that I need a doctor for my left eye."

Padre Pio said: "No, you already have received the grace we prayed for. Even though you go to Rome, your sight won't improve any more than it is now."

Nevertheless, I went to the hospital again, only in obedience to Padre Raffaele. I stayed in the hospital for thirty-two days. I told the doctor not to put any medicine in my eye. I told him only to bring me cold water, because the eye itself wasn't damaged. Only my face was burned by the blasting powder. They put atropine in the eye, but they didn't operate. Now I can't see out of my left eye. I can see only with my eye which was miraculously healed. They ruined my left eye.

On April 8, my son Francesco was born. When I came to the church on Holy Saturday for the baptism, Padre Pio said: "Greetings! Thanks be to God! Our Lady of Grace and St. Lucy have raised you from the dead!"

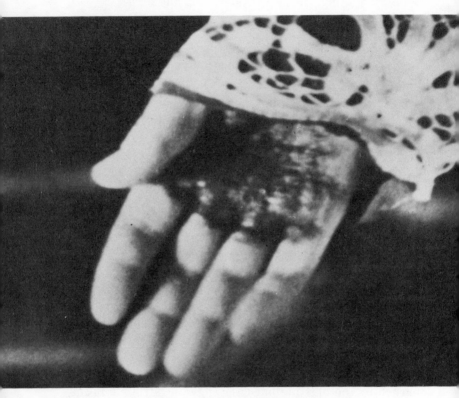

The wounds of Padre Pio's hands were about as big as a penny, but often the blood seeped across the entire palms. (Photo courtesy Casa Abresch)

Pain etched Padre Pio's features
especially during the celebration
of the Mass. (Photo courtesy Casa
Abresch)

Padre Pio wore brown, fingerless mittens during the day to
conceal the wounds and absorb
the blood. (Photo courtesy Casa
Abresch)

During Mass Padre Pio was completely absorbed with the presence and sacrifice of the Lord. (Photo courtesy Casa Abresch)

Pope Paul VI said of Padre Pio: "He was a marked representative of the stigmata of Our Lord." (Photo courtesy Casa Abresch)

INTERVIEW WITH GIUSEPPE SCATIGNA
Palermo, Sicily
June 27, 1971

In 1968, a red spot developed in my groin. It troubled me more and more, but the doctors thought it was only an impacted gland. It was very painful, and it didn't go away. But they couldn't see any injury or infection which had produced it. My wife and I went to Lourdes and asked the Blessed Mother and Padre Pio to cure me of this impacted gland.

The doctors prescribed the application of salves to the infected part, with compresses, injections, cortisone, and other medication. But the gland, rather than remaining the same or improving or becoming less swollen, increased in size and hardness, causing me severe pain.

Thirty days after Padre Pio died (Author's note: Padre Pio died on September 23, 1968), the doctor said that an operation was necessary. On October 23, 1968, they opened my groin and learned that they had been completely wrong in their diagnosis. There was a tumor, which they should not have touched, but they removed it. It was as big as a lemon, but they were not sure that it was malignant.

The operation took a long time because of the depth which had to be reached to remove the network.

After the operation, they learned that it was malignant, one of the most terrible forms of cancer, metastasis melanoma.

When cancer arrives at the point of metastasis, it is the last stage and is beyond hope.

The doctors sent me home from the hospital even before the incision had closed, because they thought I would die. They tried to hide the real truth from me, but I understood that they were lying. I realized that if they were sending me home in that condition, there was no hope for me. My whole abdomen was in tremendous pain. Everything was paralyzed. I was very thin and had the color of a person in the last days of cancer. I couldn't eat anything or stay in one position.

My brother-in-law finally told my wife the truth. He told her that my condition was hopeless. He said that if we believed in Padre Pio, we should ask his intercession, because only a miracle could cure me.

So my wife asked me: "Do you want to go to Padre Pio's hospital?"

I said: "I understand. You don't want to take me to Padre Pio's hospital, but to Padre Pio himself, because only a miracle can cure me." We went to San Giovanni Rotondo.

At the hospital, Dr. DeLuca told me: "I am receiving you only out of charity, because a man in your condition isn't supposed to stay here. There is nothing we can do for you."

The doctors told my wife: "Since you have no sons and daughters, you will be the only one to cry for him when he dies. The only thing we can do for him is X-ray every part of his body, to see if the metastasis is also in the upper part of the body. But we can do nothing else for your husband."

My wife kept going back and forth between the hospital and the church. All the time she was crying and crying and couldn't stop crying. One time when she was in front of the church, a beggar-woman came up and asked her for something, and showed her that her shoes were completely worn-out and torn. My wife gave the lady some money. As my wife walked away, the begger told her: "Don't worry, Padre Pio will grant you the grace." She immediately turned around to see the beggar, but she didn't see anybody. She kept looking for her. She never saw her again.

This little girl here, Rosaria, is my niece. She was

born during the earthquake in Sicily, and we are raising her. She calls us Daddy and Mommy. I kept saying: "I don't mind dying, but it is very painful for me not to see this little child grow up."

While I was in the hospital and my wife was praying at the tomb of Padre Pio, I had a very short vision of Padre Pio holding my niece by the hand, as if they were both walking away from me. I saw only their backs.

Another day while she was praying in the crypt and I was in the hospital, I had another very short vision. I saw Padre Pio trying to lift an enormous boulder. Young people stood around, laughing at him, saying: "How can he lift this tremendous block of stone? It is impossible. He can't even get it off the ground."

I told my wife: "You see, Padre Pio can't do anything for us, because we're not asking for a miracle. We are asking for the Resurrection. It is impossible to obtain what we are asking for."

My wife went to the superior, Padre Carmelo, of San Giovanni in Galdo, and asked him please to say a prayer in common with the friars. Padre Carmelo was so touched by all the tragedy that he went to Padre Pio's room and brought her a piece of cloth which Padre Pio had used. He said: "What I am doing is absolutely forbidden. But take this, and go to your husband and put it on the sick part of his body."

She was so happy that she took the cloth to the hospital and put it on my body where I had my last operation.

Dr. DeLuca completed the X-rays and told my wife: "The X-rays are in your husband's room, but please don't show them to him."

She asked him: "Why not? What are the results? Maybe there is nothing wrong."

"No," he said, "please don't do it. Your husband, I repeat, has only two days to live. You shouldn't give him this pain."

Then the doctor took more X-rays, and this time he

was puzzled. "I don't know, but these X-rays show that there is nothing wrong. I can't see anything wrong."

"Oh," my wife said, "that means that Padre Pio has finally worked the miracle."

He told her: "Look, I'm only a doctor. I'm not a saint."

She said: "Please tell me what I'm supposed to do. I'm not talking to you as a doctor but as a brother."

The doctor said: "In the condition in which I see your husband, there is nothing I can do. It is too late. So don't take him to another hospital, even if it is an excellent hospital. But if you have all this Faith in your heart, just take your husband and go home."

The doctor went straight to my room and asked me how I felt. I told him that I felt perfectly well. For the moment, he forgot that I had been so sick and he asked me: "Are you sure? Do you think it is possible for you to get up?"

"Of course I can," I told him.

"Do you think it is possible for you to go home?"

"Of course it is possible to go home," I told him. "I feel perfectly well."

"All right," the doctor said, "take your suitcases and go home." We left. It was November 13, 1968.

The first thing we did was to go to the convento and thank the superior. My wife told him: "Father, if it is true that my husband is completely cured, as we think, I have made a promise to give a million lire ($1,600.00) toward Padre Pio's canonization. I'll bring the money as soon as I go home and return."

Padre Carmelo answered her: "I don't have any doubt about the cure of your husband through the intercession of Padre Pio, but what I'd like is that you show everybody that this was a real miracle through Padre Pio." He told her that the only thing she should do for the moment was to keep the Faith which she had in her heart and go home with me. He said: "You have more Faith than ten nuns put together."

We returned to Palermo. Many times my wife and I asked each other if either had had a dream about Padre Pio. We were looking for a sign from him that all the danger was over and that the miracle was real.

Since my return from the hospital, I have never taken any medication. I'm completely well. My weight is the same. I've even gained a little. My work is on the farm, and it's hard. I have had many medical examinations since November 1968, but they are all negative.

The doctor at the first hospital I went to is an atheist, and my wife had a hard time getting the biopsy, which will prove that I had metastasis melanoma. Finally she got it. Now we are trying to get an affidavit from the doctor. This is very important.

I was born on March 11, 1923.

Author's note: I will spare my readers an additional "unbelievable but true" chapter which I could write on how I met the Scatignas. Nor will I speculate on the significance of my seeing a beggar-lady in the same place Mrs. Scatigna saw her. The lady disappeared on me, too, and nobody else seems to have seen her at all.

Nor will I elaborate on a "sign" which the Scatignas were looking for from Padre Pio. But I believe with them that Padre Pio gave them one of his signs, by appearing to Rosaria when she was only twenty-two months old. Rosaria said that she had seen him. A priest in Palermo, who works with little children all day long, tried hard to debunk her story, but he became convinced that she was telling the truth. I also believe that Padre Pio gave a sign to another niece. But I will not go into that.

After my interview with the Scatignas, I started to walk up the rather steep half mile along the Viale Cappuccini to Our Lady of Grace Convento. Giuseppe seized my heavy suitcase and accompanied me up the hill. As I huffed and puffed to keep up with him, I could only think

how remarkable it was that three years ago he was given
only two days to live.

INTERVIEW WITH LAURINO COSTA
San Giovanni Rotondo, Italy
July 16, 1971

I was living with my family in Padua. I had never
heard anything about Padre Pio. A friend of mine came
to my home and told me that he had been to see Padre
Pio. He gave me Padre Pio's address and a small photograph. I was tremendously impressed by the picture. I
put it in my pocket, and at night I would often dream of
him.

Well, I thought, I might as well write to Padre Pio
and ask his blessing to help me find a job. I sent a telegram and soon received a telegram in reply, telling me to
leave for San Giovanni Rotondo immediately. My friend
had given me the picture on Monday. The following Friday I left for San Giovanni Rotondo.

I had never seen Padre Pio before, and he had never
seen me. But when I arrived, he recognized me among so
many people. He called out to me: "Laurino, come,
come. I see you have arrived. Now go and feed my sick."

"But Padre," I said, "I'm not a cook. I've never
cooked before. I don't know how."

Again he said: "Go and feed my sick." I told him
that in that case he would have to teach me. He repeated:
"Go, for I'll always be near you."

I started to work that same day. It was February 14,
1958. I was thirty years old. As soon as I entered the hospital, I had the sensation that I had been there before. I
felt as though cooking had always been my trade. Nothing seemed strange or new to me, and there wasn't anything I didn't recognize. There was no doubt in my mind
that I could do the cooking. I had the feeling that I had

always lived in the hospital. I went ahead right away and did the cooking.

I like my work very much. There is a lot of work. You know, we have eight hundred people to feed. I cook for the sick, the Sisters, the doctors, for everybody. I am happy here. It is true that it is very hot here, but I feel that Padre Pio is very close to me.

Padre Pio wanted me to send for my family, but I didn't want my family to come here. We lived in the northern part of Italy, and we are used to a different way of living. We think differently. We have different ways. When I first arrived here, I wanted to turn back immediately. I didn't like it here at all. However, Padre Pio insisted that I stay. As a matter of fact, he wanted me never to leave the hospital, not even for a vacation. So I sent for my family. They came, and we settled here. That was fourteen years ago.

After working in the hospital for two or three years, I told him that I wanted to go up north to see my mother and father. He said: "Go, but come back quickly." Just before he died, I had some days off which were due to me, and I told him that I wanted to go up north again. This time he said: "No!" Then he relented and said: "How many days do you intend to be away?" When I told him that I would be away seven or eight days, he said: "I'll give you five days."

You ask me what is the importance of Padre Pio to those who have never met him personally. I have a daughter who is severely retarded. I wanted to send her away to a school, but Padre Pio advised me against it and told me that I should keep her at home. He told me that when she grew up, she would either die or get better. I guess this was a grace that even Padre Pio . . . I always pray . . . I am resigned.

It is a cross that Padre Pio has sent us, and we have learned to carry it. Who knows? If this cross were taken away from us, perhaps we'd receive a bigger one. So let us keep the one we have. It is a cross, but God has given us the strength to carry it.

Padre Pio was such a wonderful person. I'm staying here voluntarily, because he is really present here. I know he'd be near me wherever I go, but he never wanted me to leave this hospital. I can't take advantage of his death and leave now when he cannot say anything to me. He loved me very much.

Nobody should have doubts. I can tell you, in Padre Pio there is really nothing to doubt. We may all have doubts once in awhile, but we shouldn't, because of his sanctity, his honesty, and his exactness. I think he was a saint.

INTERVIEW WITH AGNESE STUMPF
Voghera, Italy
August 8, 1971

For many years I had known of Padre Pio through my aunt. I always prayed to him, and he helped me in my school work and all through the day. About two years ago I felt a pain in my knee. The doctor told me it was arthritis and gave me an injection and pills. The pain kept coming and going.

One day I twisted my ankle. The pain was so sharp. Again I went to the doctor and he took an X-ray. The results showed a tumor. At the advice of my family doctor in Voghera, I went to an orthopedist in Tartodi, Dr. Revotti.

He confirmed that I had a tumor on my knee and insisted on an operation right away. But I had no intention of being operated on. I went to Milan, to Dr. Poli. He told me the same thing: I had to be operated on. That was December 22, 1967.

I told my father and brother that I would go and ask Padre Pio if I should be operated on. I arrived at San Giovanni Rotondo on Christmas Eve and went to confession to him. I told him my troubles, and he said: "Go ahead and have the operation. Don't be afraid. I'll assist you with my prayers."

On January 2, I entered the hospital in Tartodi to be operated on. I spent the whole month of January in the hospital. The operation was a success. I returned home.

For two months I went to Tartodi for check-ups. The doctors took more X-rays and they found everything fine. They took the cast off my leg and put on a bandage and gave me exercises to do.

Then the pains came back again. Dr. Revotti took a piece of bone from my knee and sent it to Pavia for laboratory tests. The results showed that cancer had entered my blood stream. Dr. Revotti said that he wanted to amputate my leg to save my life.

The bone was all eaten up and looked like a black sponge. I couldn't stand on my left leg. The bone couldn't support me. The bone was full of pus.

Between January and October another tumor developed in the same place. The second tumor was worse than the first. It had entered my blood stream. The doctors wanted to amputate my leg before the cancer should get any worse and spread through my body.

I said No. I didn't want another operation. I left Dr. Revotti and went home. The doctor was angry with me because I didn't even say goodbye. I began a novena to Padre Pio and was willing to accept whatever he said I should do. Even if they had to amputate my leg, I'd accept that word from Padre Pio because I would know that it was for my benefit.

My father and uncle and all my family wanted me to go to another doctor. So in December I went to Dr. Carnacchia for a check-up. He said he'd never amputate the leg. He said he would replace the damaged bone, although the leg would remain stiff. I was sure that Padre Pio would help me.

In May I went to Milan, to another doctor. This doctor consulted with other doctors and they agreed that I needed another operation. I refused the operation and went back home. I was able to walk with a cane.

Then I went to Dr. Ficola, in Padre Pio's hospital. My leg was in a partial cast. Dr. Ficola also suggested an operation which would give me partial use of my knee. I didn't accept that. No operation! All of this went on from January 1969 to 1970. In the meantime I kept praying to Padre Pio. One night I dreamed of him. It seemed that I went to him using a cane, my leg in a cast. He received me in a room where he spoke to visitors. In my dream, I told him that my leg was in pain and in a cast. He looked at me and smiled, and then he raised his eyes. I kissed his hands, but he didn't have any stigmata. There were no cuts or blood on his hands.

Padre Pio was laughing. There were so many people in this room. He took me by the arm and led me to a corner, where we talked. I don't remember what he told me, but I said: "Look, Padre, I left my cane and crutches in the corner and I'm walking toward the door without them."

I'm a heavy person and I couldn't do anything without my crutches. In my dream I saw myself walking without them. I told Padre Pio: "I'm going to go back to get my crutches and my cane."

He said: "What are you going to do with them? You don't need them." With that I woke up. I could walk without my crutches.

After a year and a half in a cast, I walked a little every day with a cane for support, and then without a cane. Now I don't use it at all.

When I began to walk again, I went to Dr. Ficola in San Giovanni Rotondo. He took X-rays and said that the bone was normal. He made a statement that the damaged bone was now a normal, healthy bone. He asserted that it was a miracle. I went to Tartodi, to Dr. Revotti, who had treated me. He was surprised and said the same thing: "It is a miracle."

They took more X-rays and all agreed that it was a miracle. The doctor called in all the other doctors in the hospital and said it was a miracle.

INTERVIEW WITH MARGHERITA HAMILTON
Rome, Italy
June 17, 1971

Nothing very great ever happened to me personally, but what did happen was surely strange. The second time I went to San Giovanni Rotondo it was Eastertime. We had to stay at a rooming house, because there was no room in the one hotel that was there at the time. Everything was dirty. It was a terrible place.

We never opened our luggage. We didn't sleep in the bed. We put a big cover on the bed and slept on it. We never opened our things. Clarice said: "I want to get something out of my suitcase."

I told her: "Don't you dare take anything out in this filth and grease, because the bugs will be running around." She didn't open any luggage.

The next day was Easter Sunday. It is our custom that the first thing we eat on Easter Day is blessed hard boiled eggs. All the time I grumbled and kept saying: "For the first time in my life I won't be able to eat blessed eggs on Easter Day."

We got up at 4:00 to go to Mass at 5:00. My friend had once told Padre Pio: "The best thing you can do is say Mass at 3:00. Then we can all go to Mass and then to bed."

He answered: "Then when will you do penance?"

After Mass we were very happy. I had a big coat on. Suddenly, as we walked, I felt something in my pocket. "What do we have here?" I wondered. I didn't feel anything in my pocket when I went to church. I put my hand in my pocket and found two boiled eggs.

I told Clarice: "You put them there."

She said: "I didn't prepare any eggs, so I don't know how I could have put them there."

The same afternoon we found two good rooms elsewhere. Only then did I open my valise. I hadn't opened it before, and I hadn't given a second thought to the lunch which my maid Pasquelina had packed. When I opened my luggage, I found a little package with six sandwiches and another little parcel with four eggs. But the strange thing was that the parcel was completely sealed with a well-tied ribbon, and it was clear that there had been six eggs in the box. Only four were left. The other two were those that Padre Pio had blessed and put in my pocket. Nobody can take two eggs out of a tied box without opening it.

Another story is the one about the rose. My friend Giovanna was staying with me in my house. On the terrace was a magnificent rose, really a splendid rose. We went out onto the terrace, and Giovanna said: "Give me that rose."

"No," I said, "this is the first rose on the arbor, so you can't have this one. This one goes to the Madonna."

The next day another rose was open. I cut it and gave it to her. She told me to give it to Padre Pio. On a little table there was a photograph of Padre Pio. So I took a small vase and put the rose in it. A friend who was visitng us said: "Oh, how pale Padre Pio looks. I hope he isn't ill."

I told her: "No, it isn't that he is pale. It is only that the rose is a very deep color." I took the rose away and said: "Look, he is quite normal." She agreed. I took the rose and put it back into its place.

Suddenly one of my friends said: "B . . . b . . . but . . . but . . ."

I asked her: "What are you saying?"

The . . . the . . . the rose . . . is not there!"

I said: "But I put it there."

"Yes, I know," she said.

"Maybe it fell," Giovanna said. Giovanna had been ill and had gone to bed, but we even got her out of bed to see if it had fallen onto the bed. It had disappeared completely. It was no longer there. "It seems that Padre Pio has accepted it," Giovanna said.

Almost twenty days later, we went to San Giovanni Rotondo. We went straight to Padre Pio and met him in a small visitors' room. He had a red rose in his hand. He had the rose, *the* rose in his hand. "Thank you very much for the rose," he said. "I appreciate it very much."

Giovanna said: "Father, give it to me."

He answered: "Yes, I'll give it to you." Now the rose is framed and is in Giovanna's home.

A year after his death, I was with a friend in San Remo. I said to her: "Let's go to France today."

"It's too late to go very far," she answered. So we decided to go just as far as Monte Carlo or Cannes or Nice or wherever we wanted.

When we were near Port San Louis, the town nearest the border, I suddenly got thirsty, so thirsty I could hardly speak any more. I said to my friend: "Olga, please stop. Stop as soon as you can when you see some place where we can go in and drink something. I'm thirsty, and it's terrible."

After that I didn't say anything more. My mouth was completely dry. I couldn't understand that, because never in my life did that happen. Never. I never stop. When I go away, I go to the place I'm going to. If I have to drive five hours, I drive five hours, but I never stop.

In front of us was a big yellow moving van. Then came our car. I joked with my friend: "What beautiful sightseeing here!" The only thing which we saw was the enormous truck which we were following.

Finally, when we were almost at Port San Louis, we came to a place where we could turn off and leave the car. There was a café and souvenir shop. We got out of the car and were walking toward the café, when suddenly there was a terrible bang. I said: "It's a bomb." Olga thought it might be a mine that had exploded.

We went into the café. Then the proprietor came in, and I asked him if someone had thrown a bomb. He told me: "Oh no, madam. There was another big truck in back of the moving van that you were following. It's brakes were gone, and it went straight down the hill into the other truck."

If we had continued on, if I hadn't been thirsty, we would have been squashed between those two big trucks. When the man told us what happened, I said instantly: "I see the hand of Padre Pio." First of all there was the crash. Then my thirst was completely gone. As soon as I got into the café, my friend asked me what I wanted to drink. I told her I really didn't want anything, but I said that I had better drink something, because I was the one who made us stop. My thirst had gone away instantly.

You ask me why I saw the hand of Padre Pio in this. Padre Pio always protected us. When I returned to Rome, my friend Giovanna came rushing to embrace me.

"It's a miracle that you see me again," I said to her.

"I know," she answered me.

"You can't know it," I told her. "I haven't told anyone about it."

"I know it," she repeated. "I had a dream of Padre Pio, and I asked him how you were. "Oh," he said, "Margherita! You can thank me, because if it hadn't been for me, you would never see her again." He told her that. She couldn't possibly have known about it any other way.

Twice Padre Pio did extraordinary things for me. For thirty-five years I suffered from spastic rhinitis. It doesn't kill you, but it is an inflammation that takes away all the pleasures of life. It isn't always present. In my case I felt it every morning of my life for a long time.

When I woke up, I started sneezing, and didn't stop for two or three hours. My face was swollen. I generally used seventeen big men's handkerchiefs every morning. My family brought me all over the world to see doctors, but nobody knew what it was. It really damaged my life. Many times I could have been married, but I didn't want to marry. It was impossible. If I had a child, and that child began to sneeze, I would be desperate. I didn't want that.

After awhile I grew a little better, and I had my attacks only once every two days. Sometimes the seizure lasted for a long time, but then it stopped. It wasn't continuous any longer.

I went to Padre Pio to ask him to pray for my sister-in-law and my aunt, both of whom had cancer. He said: "My daughter, it is a terrible illness. We must pray together for their souls." I knew he could not cure them.

I came out of the confessional and knelt before him. He put both his hands on my head. It was such a weight that I had the impression that my neck was going into my shoulders. I never had another sneezing attack again. If I go near a window, I sneeze, that's all. But I have never had another attack.

How can I judge if he cured me? It is something I can't prove. I was already better than I had been in many years. It was the same when he saved my life on the way to Monte Carlo. Giovanna could have dreamed it. I don't know how to prove it, but I know it was he.

Another time Padre Pio helped was when I had influenza. I had an abscess in my ear, and I was absolutely deaf. I wrote to my friend Mrs. Sanguinetti, and I told her that I was confined to bed for a long time. "God's will be done," I wrote. But I couldn't hide my hope that I would not remain deaf.

Mrs. Sanguinetti went to Padre Pio and read my letter to him. At first he didn't say anything. When she was going away, he told her, "Look here, tell Margherita that I'll pray that her hearing won't be taken away from her."

If the tympanum (ear drum) breaks, it takes twenty-one days to heal. After twenty-one days I could hear perfectly well again and I didn't think anything more about it.

Finally, Giovanna and I were traveling about, and I learned of a place in Sinione, on Lake Ganda, where they cure hearing defects. I said that I would go there, because if my hearing should go later on, I didn't want to make Padre Pio work for me. I said that not in the sense that I didn't want to be helped by him, but I didn't want him to give something of himself. We all know these things are obtained through his penance.

The doctor looked at me, and the first thing he said was: "You can't hear from this ear."

I said: "No, I can hear."

"No," he answered, "you hear from the other one, and you think you hear from this one."

"But I also hear from the other one," I told him.

He said: "That's impossible. An audio test will tell the truth."

He tested both of my ears, and the results proved that my two ears were almost exactly alike. The one that had been very bad, my left ear, was just a little bit poorer than the other.

"What do we have here?" the doctor said. "I don't understand it. Let me look at it again." So he looked at my ear again.

"You can't hear," he told me, "because you have so many inflammations of the ear drum. Every time the inflammation punctures the ear drum, it makes a scar. After awhile the cicatrization gets hard, and the drum can no longer vibrate. Your drum can no longer vibrate, because it is full of these things. I don't understand how you hear."

Suddenly I remembered what Padre Pio had told Mrs. Sanguinetti, that he would pray that my hearing would remain. I told the doctor, "Padre Pio did this."

He said to me: "When you come with these reasons, there is nothing I can say." So I went away, and that was all. But I know that I hear because Padre Pio prayed for me.

Author's note: I interviewed Miss Hamilton in her home in Rome. At the time, she was eighty-one years old. She is one of the most mentally alert people I know. She exudes kindness and graciousness, in the most honest and the very best sense of those words. She spoke with enthusiasm, with vigor. Yet, her spirit is calm and serene, at the opposite pole from anything fanatical or hysterical. She is simply a grand old lady, absolutely happy and at peace with herself and with the world. I saw in her what love, a deep, all-absorbing love for a priest, her Spiritual Father, and his for her, should mean.

CHAPTER 12

Bilocation

On the Feast of Corpus Christi, June 12, 1952, Lucia Bellodi was lying on her death bed. Suddenly she smiled, opened her eyes, sat up in bed and began to wave her arms as if overcome with joy. She cried out: "Padre Pio told me that I am cured in the name of God. He told me to get up and come immediately to his monastery because he wants to bless me and thank God with me."

Lucia was the daughter of a farmer in Mirandola, Italy. At the age of fourteen she had been stricken with pernicious diabetes. For four years her parents had taken her from one hospital to another, but nobody could help her. Her condition grew more and more critical. Because no hospital would admit her, she was admitted into an old folks home run by nuns.

Her abdomen had become enormously deformed. Her thirst was insatiable. Next to her bed she had a container which held twenty-five quarts of water. She emptied that every twenty-four hours. She lost the use of speech. Drinking was her only relief, but there was no human cure.

On the Feast of Corpus Christi at about 6:00 p.m.,

she suddenly stopped drinking water and called for the Mother Superior and told her that she felt an urge to go to the chapel to pray. The Mother Superior feared that the girl was delirious. But Lucia insisted and asked her to bring only one glass of water.

"Padre Pio came to see me," Lucia told the nun. "He told me that I will die soon, because I cannot be cured." Lucia had misunderstood Padre Pio. He had told her only that the doctors could not cure her.

The nuns took her to the chapel. While there, Lucia drank no water. She refused to touch even the glass which the Mother Superior took along. She prayed for a few moments, and then she fainted. Taking her back to her little room, they called the chaplain. Everyone thought that she was about to die. But then she awakened and sprang out of bed completely cured.

On June 17, she visited San Giovanni Rotondo with two of the nuns. When she met Padre Pio, he smiled, blessed her and said: "I have been waiting for you."

Father Dominic Meyer, Padre Pio's secretary, told me of another lady, an Austrian, who was cured by Padre Pio. Seven years previously she had been so captivated by Padre Pio's life and spirit that she moved to San Giovanni Rotondo. But she paid a price for the move, not so much in terms of money, but in sacrifice. She was all alone and very depressed. Also, for six weeks her arm had been so swollen that she could not so much as move a chair or make her bed.

One evening Padre Pio appeared to her in a dream. He pressed his thumbs in to her arm. In the morning the arm was completely healed.

A few months later, after confession, she asked Padre Pio if it had been he who had appeared to her and cured her. "*Sì,*" he answered, "Yes."

In World War II, during the North African Campaign, an Italian regiment was being fiercely shelled by the Allies. One of the Italian soldiers had taken cover behind a large rock. Suddenly a "monk" as he called him, stood next to him, pulled him gently by the sleeve and told him to get out from behind the rock. The soldier refused to leave what he thought was a safe place.

The "monk" tugged on his sleeve more vigorously, but the soldier still wouldn't move. Finally the "monk" grabbed his arm and pulled him away by force. At that very moment, a shell exploded where they had been standing and devastated the whole area. The soldier was safe. The "monk" disappeared.

Some days later, the soldier told his buddy the story. His friend showed him a picture of Padre Pio, which he always carried with him. "That's the monk who saved my life," the soldier exclaimed. He had never seen nor heard of Padre Pio before.

One of Padre Pio's spiritual children, a marquise from Rome, decided to go to confession in St. Peter's Basilica. It was quite late, and the attendant told her that all the confessors had left.

She entered anyway, intending to say a prayer. Halfway through the Basilica, she met a Capuchin, who asked her: "*Signorina*, do you want to go to confession?" She accepted the invitation.

On her way out of St. Peter's, the attendant suggested that she return early the following morning. "No," she said, "I have already gone to confession."

"How?" he asked her, and made a gesture implying that she was out of her mind.

Many years passed. The marquise visited San Giovanni Rotondo with two lady-friends. Padre Pio walked straight up to her and said: "I know you."

"Padre," she answered, "this is the first time I've been here."

"Don't you remember me," he asked, "from St. Peter's when I met you?"

Another of his spiritual daughters was Madre Teresa Salvadores, the Superior of the Escuela Medalla Milagrosa, in Montevideo, Uruguay. In bitter pain, she was at the point of death from cancer of the stomach and lesions of the arteries of her heart.

The nuns of her community wrote to Padre Pio, imploring his help. According to their calculations, the same day on which Padre Pio received the letter, a lady, a relative of Monsignor Damiani, the Vicar General of the Diocese of Salto, returned from Italy and gave Madre Teresa one of Padre Pio's gloves.

Let Madre Teresa tell her own story.

"The glove was applied to the side where I had a swelling the size of a fist, and to my throat where I felt I was suffocating. Then I fell asleep. In a dream I saw Padre Pio, who touched my side where the pain was. . . . It is a fact that after three hours I woke up. I asked for my habit, so that I could get out of bed where I had been lying for months.

"I got up without the help of anyone and went down to the chapel. At noon I went to the dining room. For months I had not attempted to eat, but then I ate more than any of my companions. From that day, I have felt nothing." She immediately took up her usual activities, completely cured.

Dr. Gianbattista Morelli, Professor at the University of Montevideo, was her attending physician. After six months he and two other doctors examined her and declared her to be completely healed.

The Vicar General himself, Monsignor Damiani, also experienced the help of Padre Pio through bilocation. The details of the story are told by Cardinal Barbieri, at present the retired Cardinal Archbishop of Montevideo.

Monsignor Damiani had been a frequent visitor to San Giovanni Rotondo. "I want to die here," he told Padre Pio. "I want to retire here and die here, so that you can assist me on my death bed."

"No," Padre Pio told him, "you will die in Uruguay. You have an obligation to return to your diocese."

"Then promise me," the Monsignor demanded, "that you will assist me at the hour of my death."

Padre Pio hesitated a moment, seemingly lost in thought, and then answered: "Yes, I promise."

In 1941, Monsignor Damiani attended a meeting in Salto, with the Papal Nuncio and the Bishops of Uruguay. They all stayed at the Bishop's residence, where Monsignor Damiani also resided.

One night, Cardinal Barbieri was awakened by someone knocking on his door. When he was fully awake, he noticed that his door was half open, and he saw a Capuchin passing by. He couldn't see the Capuchin's face.

The Cardinal got up, dressed, and went to the room of Monsignor Damiani. The Monsignor had had an attack of angina pectoris and was dying. The Cardinal summoned the other Bishops, and they all returned to Monsignor Damiani's room. They remained with him until he died.

On the Monsignor's desk the Cardinal found a slip of paper on which Monsignor Damiani had written in Italian: "Padre Pio came."

Cardinal Barbieri wished to verify for himself the identity of the person who had aroused him out of sleep. The next time he visited San Giovanni Rotondo, he asked Padre Pio if it had been he. The Padre gave an evasive answer. The Cardinal pressed him for a direct answer, but Padre Pio did not want to say expressly that it had been he, nor would he deny it.

The Cardinal laughed and said: "I understand." Padre Pio nodded affirmatively.

Then the Cardinal asked Padre Pio if he would assist him on his death bed. Padre Pio said that he, Padre Pio, would die before the Cardinal, but that he would assist him from heaven.

Padre Pio's gift of bilocation poses more questions than a curious biographer can find the answers to. What actually happened? How can a person explain it? How did Padre Pio explain it?

According to Pietruccio, the blind spiritual son of Padre Pio whom everyone in San Giovanni Rotondo knows, Padre Pio "disappeared" many times from the confessional. Then he would be seen perhaps an hour later, in the convento or in the church, as though nothing extraordinary had happened.

Padre Pio's confessional was conspicuous, and Padre Pio was conspicuous in it. Also, it was always surrounded by a throng of devotees and penitents. Padre Pio *could not* leave the confessional without being seen. Yet, he disappeared from the confessional.

Once his friends asked him where he went. "I flew over your heads," he answered them.

"Maybe he was joking," Pietruccio told me, "but the people didn't see him leave, and I didn't see him leave. The people think he went away by bilocation." Padre Pio told Pietruccio that he went away because he wasn't able to breathe. Pietruccio became blind only in 1925. Therefore, he had known Padre Pio for eight years before he lost his sight.

Maybe the scientists from Duke University, in their studies of extrasensory perception and related strange phenomena, can interview the people who were eyewitnesses to these events and piece together the physical events which actually happened during Padre Pio's bilocation. Unfortunately, it is already too late to interview Padre Pio himself on this.

One day Padre Onorato and Padre Alberto saw Padre Pio lean out of a window, and they heard him say the words of absolution for confession: "I absolve you of your sins. . . ." A few days later some people from Morcone came to San Giovanni Rotondo to thank Padre Pio for having assisted a dying man, just at the time he had spoken the words of absolution. But Padre Pio had never left his convento.

Padre Alessio, who tended Padre Pio's every need morning and night, said that he had never heard Padre

Pio speak about bilocation. But he told me of one strange incident which he himself had witnessed, similar to the experience of Padre Onorato and Padre Alberto.

"One day," Padre Alessio said, "I was in his room, sitting in the armchair. Padre Pio was in bed. Both of us were fully awake. I could hear him praying the rosary. I, too, was praying the rosary. Then all of a sudden he stopped, and I heard him say: 'Come here. What do you want?'

"Again after a few seconds, he said: 'Come here. What do you want?'

"Then in a more insistent tone, he said: 'Come here! What do you want!'

"Then I heard him pronounce the words of absolution: 'I absolve you of your sins. . . . For your penance, you will say five Our Fathers, and five Hail Marys and five Glory be to the Fathers.' Then he was silent."

Another time, Padre Alessio asked him jokingly when they would go to Lourdes. Padre Pio replied: "I don't have to go to Lourdes. I go there every night. I see Our Lady of Lourdes every night."

The friars who lived with Padre Pio were not gullible. One of them told me of a time he was with Padre Pio, when suddenly Padre Pio started to hear someone's confession. "I didn't see anyone," the Brother told me, "but then he gave absolution. I thought he was going out of his mind."

"I could never understand that," the Brother continued, "until I heard the explanation that he had gone in bilocation to hear someone's confession. At the same time it seemed that he was having a great struggle with someone. He was sort of bouncing and turning and at the same time carrying on this dialogue: 'How long . . . and what else . . . and what else. . . .' "

One day after Padre Pio's death, Padre Fortunato was walking down the corridor of the convento in San Giovanni Rotondo, when he saw Padre Pio just ahead of him. "Padre Pio, wait for me," he called out. But Padre Pio disappeared. This was no case of mistaken identity. They had lived together in the same house for many years. If Padre Fortunato actually had seen someone else, where did he disappear to?

A man from Rome, highly respected by the friars, told them that once when he had been suffering from extreme grief, Padre Pio visited him in his home in Rome. However, we repeat that from 1918 until his death in 1968, Padre Pio never left San Giovanni Rotondo.

When Padre Eusebio was first assigned to San Giovanni Rotondo, he was totally unimpressed by the claims of Padre Pio's stigmata and bilocation and miracles. But he decided to investigate these claims. He asked Padre Pio if it were true that he had visited the man in Rome. Padre Pio answered him: "How is that possible? I have not left the friary for so many years. And Rome? Why I haven't been there since the time I accompanied my sister there to become a nun."

"But Padre," Padre Eusebio pressed him, "he insists that you have been in his home. He says that he saw you."

Padre Pio realized that he could not escape this line of questioning.

"Oh, that is another matter," he said. "When these things happen, the Lord permits only that person to see, and only for that moment. Nobody else can see. Otherwise, how many miracles would the Lord have to work?"

One evening when he was assisting Padre Pio to go to bed, Padre Eusebio said to him: "*Bon voyage,* Padre." Padre Pio answered him: "Thanks."

Padre Eusebio added: "You should ask my permission when you go flying around during the night."

Padre Pio replied: "I once asked the person whom it was my duty to ask. That is sufficient."

"But Padre," Padre Eusebio asked, "why don't you

take me with you? I'll tie my cord to yours, and we will fly together?''

Padre Pio answered him: "Then what will you do if we are up high and your cord becomes untied?'' Padre Eusebio didn't pursue the conversation.

We have another significant insight into Padre Pio's gift of bilocation from the questions which Dr. Sanguinetti asked him.

"When God sends a saint, for instance St. Anthony,'' the doctor asked, "to another place by bilocation, is the saint aware of what is happening?''

Padre Pio answered him: "One moment he is here, and the next moment he is where God wants him.''

"But is he really in two places at once?''

"Yes.''

"How is this possible?''

"By a prolongation of his personality.''

With that, we will leave the experts in parapsychology to probe as much as they care into Padre Pio's preternatural gifts. The Church has always welcomed and used scientific inquiry before making any decision on such matters. In the case of bilocation, scientific inquiry cannot do much more than prove that Padre Pio was actually present in two places at one time. For any further knowledge, even with regard to Padre Pio's statement about "a prolongation of his personality,'' scientists must admit that they are faced with a reality which is beyond their competency to explore or explain. At that point, the Church stands alone with the right and ability to judge the facts.

As a postscript to this chapter, I'd like to add a word about my attempt to visit Cardinal Mindszenty in June, 1971. At that time he was living in the U.S. Embassy, in Budapest, Hungary. He had been brought there in 1956 by the Hungarian Freedom Fighters, who had regained their city from the Communists and held control for a few hours.

I wanted to verify directly from Cardinal Mindszenty a story that I had heard secondhand from a most reliable source in the Vatican. When the Cardinal was still in a Communist jail, the account goes, before his release in 1956, Padre Pio had brought him water and wine and altar breads and a chalice for Mass, and had actually remained to serve him Mass.

At the Embassy I was not allowed to speak to the Cardinal. I was not even permitted to submit a note through someone who had access to him. My last-ditch request was that the Cardinal be asked to write one word, *Yes* or *No*, on a card, to be mailed to me if his situation should change. That request was also denied.

When the Cardinal left his protective custody at the Embassy and took up residence in Vienna, I wrote to him and asked if the story about him and Padre Pio were true. He answered me with a one-sentence letter: "I cannot say anything about that."

CHAPTER 13

Charismatic Aromas

From the time I resolved to write a book on Padre Pio, I have debated with myself whether I should make more than incidental mention of his charismatic aromas. I have never doubted that they are a conspicuous and frequent phenomenon, and as such they deserve "equal time" with his other fantastic gifts.

But I feared that a whole chapter on his charismatic aromas might be like the last straw which broke the camel's back, burdening my readers' credulity beyond the limit. I feared that finally my readers would dismiss *everything* I have said about the man as poppycock.

After mature thought, however, I have concluded that I must not play down his charismatic aromas. Instead, I must place this gift in its proper context in the whole story of his life, neither exaggerating nor minimizing it. The aromas associated with Padre Pio are too universal and too conspicuous to gloss over with as little mention as I have so far made of them. Not to tell the whole story would be a disservice to all concerned, to Padre Pio and to my readers. I feel that a whole chapter is necessary to do justice to this topic.

Many people (I believe that they could easily be numbered in the thousands) have said that they experienced an odor — they really smelled something — which was associated in some way with Padre Pio. The odor was charismatic — through it Padre Pio was telling them something, perhaps that he was nearby simply to be with them, or to thank or protect or warn them, or that he was about to obtain a miracle for them.

People who have experienced Padre Pio's charismatic aromas range from atheists to devotees. They include the clergy and laity, professional and nonprofessional people, in San Giovanni Rotondo and across the ocean. Often these people, when they smelled the aroma, were not thinking of Padre Pio. Many of them had never even heard that such a phenomenon was associated with him.

The aromas to which I refer were real odors, but never body odor. They might be the smell of roses, tobacco, incense, lavender, lilies, violets, pine, camphor, sulphur, or carbolic acid.

At least four doctors have given us written statements on this phenomenon. Two of the four doctors were Dr. Romanelli and Dr. Festa, who had been commissioned to give Padre Pio an extensive physical examination.

Doctor Romanelli wrote: "In June, 1919 (sic: it was May, 1919) on my first visit to Padre Pio, I noticed a peculiar scent, so much so that I said to Father Valenzano, who was with me at the time, that I thought it was very improper for a friar to use perfume. For the next two days, either when talking to Padre Pio or just sitting in his room, I did not notice anything. Before leaving, however, as I was going down the stairs, I had a whiff of the same odor, but only for a moment, because it soon disappeared. I have consulted several learned scientists to find their opinion of perfume in the blood. Every one of them declared that it is impossible for blood to have a sweet odor, but the blood that drips from the stigmata of Padre Pio has a characteristic scent, which even people with no sense of smell can detect. Besides, when the blood is coagulated or dried on some garment that he has worn, it still retains its perfume. This is contrary to all natural properties of blood, and yet many people have experienced it and still do experience it."

Doctor Festa has given us his own report: "The blood which is discharged in droplets from the wounds has a special perfume, fine and delicate, that many people who have approached him have distinctly noticed.

"Padre Pio never used any kind of perfume. Nevertheless, there were many people who, as they approached him, very clearly noticed the pleasant smell of violets or roses.

"As far as I am concerned, I can testify that during my first visit I took from his side a small piece of cloth stained with blood. I wanted to examine it under the microscope. I did not notice any special odor because I had been deprived of my sense of smell. However, a distinguished official and other people in the car with me as we were returning from San Giovanni very clearly noticed the special fragrance. They did not know that I had brought with me the special piece of cloth enclosed in a small case.

"They noticed this, in spite of the fact that the car was moving and air was circulating. They assured me it was exactly the same perfume that emanates from the person of Padre Pio. In Rome, during the following days, and for a long time afterwards, I kept the same cloth in a closet in my study. It filled the whole room with perfume, so much so that patients who came to consult me continually asked me how to explain it.

"My colleague Dr. Romanelli accompanied me during my second visit to Padre Pio. His sense of smell is normal. Along with a large number of people, he verified the same impression that I got from the people mentioned above."

Dr. Festa went into a lengthy analysis of the properties of blood and concluded: "This phenomenon, then, is contrary to every natural and scientific law. It goes beyond the possibility of logical discussion. But in all honesty we cannot deny the reality of its existence."

The doctor raised the question whether the perfume might possibly be the result of the tincture of iodine. He answers very definitely that that is impossible. In fact, iodine would cause a repulsive odor.

Just as Padre Pio had applied iodine in the hope of healing the wounds, so also Dr. Festa applied iodine and other medications to the wounds. As time went on, the wounds continued to discharge little drops of blood. The iodine had no effect. The smell of the iodine was usually very strong. A long time after the iodine was no longer used, drops of blood continued to come from the wounds. The perfume did not diminish in any way but continued to be equally strong.

To the testimony of Doctors Romanelli and Festa we can add the written reports of two other doctors. Dr. Amanzio Duodo, of Veglio Mosso Picco (Vercelli), wrote: "On February 15, 1950, I was with the Battista Bertolo family, of Vallemosso. We were engaged in pleasant conversation. In addition to myself, all the members of the above-mentioned family were present. . . . A friend who had recently come from San Giovanni Rotondo was describing to us the great humility of Padre Pio in spite of all the publicity about his work, when suddenly and unexpectedly an intense perfume of violets enveloped us all. It lasted about a half hour, although the doors and windows were wide open. Later on, a pungent and strong odor of perfume blanketed (literally: assailed) us."

Another doctor, Dr. Eduardo Bianco, of Vallemosso, corroborated Dr. Duodo's statement: "I, the undersigned, assert that on the occasion referred to by Dr. Duodi, I was present and smelled the odor of violets. I must add that on various other occasions I have repeatedly perceived odors of roses, violets and carnations, whose source was positively not artificial. I wish also to declare that these observations of mine elude all scientific explanation, although I have done my best to rationalize them."

Sometimes Padre Pio's charismatic aroma was sensed by people without a sense of smell. Mrs. Ann McAvoy, who lives in the Bronx, N.Y., had never heard about Padre Pio until an Augustinian priest, Father Robert E. Regan, O.S.A., mentioned him to her.

Mrs. McAvoy had been praying that tension in her family be resolved, and that her brother, Frank Stoddard, would be relieved of the severe pain of terminal cancer of the stomach, so that he might die in peace.

On November 1, 1968, Frank began to take the medication which the doctor had prescribed. On November 11, Father Regan visited him again. For the first time he told Frank and Ann about Padre Pio. He applied to Frank's stomach a crucifix which Padre Pio had blessed, and he left the crucifix with them. Afterwards, Ann applied the crucifix a few times to her brother's stomach and prayed with him. All the while, Frank did not have to take a single pill for his pain.

The following evening Ann was exhausted. "My brother was in the bedroom," Ann told me. "I was sitting on the couch and picked up the *Times*. I had not even opened it when I sensed a beautiful, sweet odor. I thought to myself: 'What is this?'

"Twenty-three years ago I had pneumonia, and ever since that time I did not have any sense of smell. But then I smelled honeysuckle. There was nothing around to give off an aroma. It got stronger and stronger. It came two or three times. Then it died away.

"I broke into a sweat, because this was unusual and

frightening. Perspiration dripped from my forehead. I thought I was losing my mind. I couldn't figure it out. I had on no makeup. I had just sat down, and there wasn't even time for the heat of the lamp to affect anything.

"I didn't connect this with Padre Pio, but it bothered me all night. I didn't tell Father Regan about it. When I told him later on, he scolded me: 'You should have told me sooner.'

"I said I didn't tell him because I didn't know how to explain it. Then for the first time he explained that frequently the aroma of flowers and incense are connected with the presence of Padre Pio.

"My brother said the rosary every day till he died. Since November 11, he said that he was very comfortable, even though he had not taken any more medication. I asked him: 'How do you feel? Do you feel any pain?'

"He answered: 'No, I don't feel any pain, but I do have a little nausea.'

"On December 6, 1968, my brother fell asleep and slept for twelve hours. He died a beautiful, peaceful death in his sleep. And peace was restored to the family, too."

Mrs. Mario Pasqualini, of San Francisco, wrote to Padre Pio to thank him for helping her daughter. "Our little girl, who is six years old," Mrs. Pasqualini wrote, "is very delicate and subject to colds leading to pneumonia and bronchitis. Last June was no exception. It was the afternoon just following her first Holy Communion, and we had prepared a little dinner to celebrate. A few friends were invited, including Mr. and Mrs. Victorio Caimotto (Padre Pio's spiritual children). Suddenly, our little girl began to complain of not feeling well. She coughed violently, vomited repeatedly and ran a temperature of 104 degrees. We called the doctor immediately, but it seemed ages before he arrived.

"In the meantime, Mrs. Caimotto suggested that we pray to Padre Pio and to our Blessed Mother. No sooner had we finished our prayer than our little girl opened her eyes and said: 'Oh, mother, I smell such a sweet smell. It's like the incense they have in church.'

"Her eyes seemed brighter, her cheeks were no longer burning with fever. By the time the doctor arrived, her temperature was almost normal. He diagnosed that she had bronchitis, but it was the mildest case she ever had."

On one occasion the aromatic sign of Padre Pio's presence almost ended in a broken marriage. Vincenzo Catalano, who lived in East Harlem, New York City, had just returned to the Sacraments after being away for sixty-four years. He makes it known very emphatically that it was Padre Pio who led him to make a good confession to a Capuchin priest at Our Lady Queen of Angels Church, on East 113th Street, in New York City.

On the way home, he bought a money order for $12.00, to send to Padre Pio. When he arrived home, he took the receipt out of his pocket and tried to tell his wife what he had done. But she didn't hear a word he said. The receipt reeked of perfume. "You have another woman!" she screamed.

Fortunately, Vincenzo was able to convince his wife that the aroma was associated with Padre Pio.

In Hazelton, Pa., Dr. James Falvello was for twelve years Chief of the Dental Staff at St. Joseph's Hospital. In 1957, he was admitted to the hospital as a patient for surgery to remove his kidney stones. His doctor performed two cystoscopies but without success. "The pain was so severe," Dr. Falvello told me, "that I felt as though the operating instruments were still in me."

He had a third and a fourth cystoscopy, neither of them any more successful than the others. When his doctor said that he would try a fifth cystoscopy, he told Dr. Falvello that if he didn't have any better results he would have to undergo open surgery on his side.

"At ten minutes to four, on the morning of June 19,"

Dr. Falvello told me, "I got out of bed. I rested my elbows on the stool that we used at that time to get out of bed. I knelt down and signed myself with the Sign of the Cross, and I said an Our Father, a Hail Mary, and a Glory Be.

"This was my petition. I said: 'Padre Pio, if you are at the holy Sacrifice of the Mass, or if you are in meditation and can hear me, won't you be so kind as to include my petition with yours, that I may be spared the open incision in my body, and may the hand of my surgeon be the divine instrument to rid me of my stone.'

"I had the cysto. I guess it was around 8:30 when I returned to my room. I was just coming out of the anesthesia, when my wife came into the room. I could see the door leading to my private room. I could see the little picture of Padre Pio which I had kissed so often, and a little piece of palm which was loaned to me by an attorney who is a devotee of Padre Pio.

"I could hear my wife walking into my room. My nurse said: 'What a strong perfume you have on!'

"Mrs. Falvello said: 'Who, me? I stayed with my widowed sister-in-law last night just two blocks from here, and I came hurriedly to see how Jim made out. I haven't used any powder or any cosmetics at all.'

"Within a few minutes the nurse came to my bedside and said to my wife: 'The smell is stronger at his bedside.'

"By this time I was worried if I was out of the anesthesia, and if I had heard them correctly. I said to them: 'I heard you talking about a strong odor.' By this time I had passed my right forefinger and thumb near my nose, and the rose perfume, which I had identified, seemed to be emitted from them. This was the hand in which I held the picture of Padre Pio so many times during the day.

"I asked the nurse, Mrs. Brill: 'Did you ever hear of Padre Pio?'

"She said: 'I never heard the name before.'

"I said: 'That's his picture on my bureau.'

"I called to my wife: 'Eileen, come over here.'

"She said: 'What do you want?'

"I said: 'Just come over here. Smell the odor of my finger and the thumb of my right hand.'

"She said: 'Where did you get that?'

"I told her that it was the perfume of Padre Pio. No one knew what I had asked for at ten minutes to four, on my knees. Only myself. I knew then that I would not have to undergo the operation, even though it was scheduled for 1:00 o'clock that afternoon.

"Shortly after that, the doctor, Louis McAllos, came in and said: 'Jim, we are canceling the 1:00 o'clock surgery.'

"All I said was: 'Thanks, Louie!' I didn't say anything to him about what was in my mind. There was little or no pain, no bleeding. I was quite comfortable. I was discharged and went home."

Another person who has spoken extensively about Padre Pio's charismatic aromas is Alberto Del Fante, who attributes his conversion from atheism to Padre Pio.

"I was coming home with my family," Del Fante wrote, "after a visit to my parents. It was Saturday, and thinking that the next day I could have a rest, I decided to write and work until three o'clock in the morning. I had previously left a certain piece of work unfinished, so now I started where I had left off, but I omitted to bless myself, as is my custom.

"I was suddenly aware of a delicate scent, which I did not at first recognize. Padre Pio's different odors do not have the quality of commercial perfume. They resemble each other but are not the same. This was the smell of incense.

"I called my wife and my children, who had already gone to bed. They all came down, including the maid, Maria Rocca. Every one of them smelled incense except my Flora. In order not to influence them, I asked them to tell me what they could smell. My wife and my oldest daughter as well as the maid said at once that it was incense. My little boy could not exactly describe it. I was most particular in not suggesting the word incense to any of them, being anxious not to give them any lead.

"Padre Pio was telling me that I had not held to my bargain with him to make the Sign of the Cross and say a prayer before starting to work. The scent remained in my room for awhile, and I was made very happy by it, feeling that I had Padre Pio near me.

"There are innumerable accounts of this kind, and it would be very worthwhile to make a study of each particular case, since each one reveals the manner in which Padre Pio follows souls, and how he guides, counsels and comforts, using this divine gift. Many of these souls are suffering from various trials, and there are those who are begging for his powerful intercession with God. There are mothers with sick children, fathers asking help in financial difficulties, people who want him to guide, support and help them. He makes them aware of his perfume to warn them not to be afraid, but to hope, to pray and to behave well. He warns them not to return to the wrong road but to steer always toward the right goal. Their spirits become serene and their hearts are filled with hope because they are no longer alone. They feel that they are sustained by a supernatural strength. Many people have been assured of their prayers being answered through the Father's perfume, and each time the scent suggests the favor that he has asked for.

"As I have said, the perfume is indescribable. It has all the varieties of ordinary odors, but it also has elements that are new and different and hitherto unknown. Sometimes it is more distinct than others, sometimes it reminds me of roses, violets or lilies, or, in fact, of any sweet-smelling flower. At other times it is like incense or carbolic acid, and again it is like some very fine oriental tobacco. This is the first kind of odor that is noticed, particularly by recent converts, and it is what I smelled the first time I went to see him.''

CHAPTER 14

The Social Works of Padre Pio

*"We are building not only the Casa
Sollievo, but also other facilities on the
whole mountain. They will be the cubs of
the lioness. They are not only my works,
but God's, just as He shows me."*

Padre Pio

All through this book we have spoken of Padre Pio's hospital, the *Casa Sollievo della Sofferenza,* the Home for the Relief of Suffering. The Casa Sollievo della Sofferenza towers above the town of San Giovanni Rotondo as the first and most conspicuous of Padre Pio's social works.

Physically, the Casa is a beautiful hospital with almost one thousand beds, providing medical services which will match any hospital in Italy and perhaps in the world.

Padre Pio didn't want it to be called a hospital. "Hospitals," he said, "are places of suffering. This is a Home for the Relief of Suffering." In it, Faith and medical practice are the twin therapies which cure the whole person. "We are not only building a hospital," he insisted, "but we are cooperating in the work of Christ's Redemption by the pains and sufferings of the people."

Capped with a heliport, the five-story, 200-foot-long center unit of the Casa is located across the piazza from the convento. Like the convento and church themselves, the Casa is slotted into the mountain which rises behind it like the back of a grizzly bear, 1,800-feet above the plains of Foggia. A triple tier of satellite buildings are also shelved into the mountain around the Casa like cubs scampering for the nursing breast.

Padre Pio first got the idea to build a hospital when tragedy after tragedy struck down the poor townsfolk. Often they died en route to the hospital in Foggia as they bumped along the fourteen miles of dirt roads in their horse-drawn or ox-drawn wagons. "I heard these sad stories time after time," he said. "I felt sorry for them."

Even in Foggia, medical care was far from perfect. Padre Pio once saw a man from San Giovanni Rotondo who had been wounded by a mine. The victim was taken to Foggia, almost bleeding to death, and was left on a cot in the corridor, because no room was available and no doctor had time to treat him.

When Padre Pio heard that after a week the man was still waiting to be treated, he decided to build a hospital in San Giovanni Rotondo.

When Padre Pio first revealed his plans for a hospital, few people agreed with his judgment. "Where will you get the money?" they asked.

Two doctors supported him, Dr. Mario Sanvico and Dr. Carlo Kiswarday. The diary of Dr. Sanvico tells us how the dream began to materialize. After their meeting in Padre Pio's room at 6:30 p.m. on June 9, 1940, Padre Pio said: "From this evening my great earthly work begins. I bless you and all those who will contribute to my work, which will be so beautiful and so great."

He appointed Dr. Kiswarday as treasurer and

pressed a gold ten franc napoleon, worth a few cents, into his hands. "I, too, want to contribute my small offering," he said.

The second contributor was no richer. Pietruccio, the blind man, contribute two lire, only a few cents.

The next entry in Dr. Sanvico's diary fills us in on Padre Pio's choice of a name: "This evening, at seven o'clock, I asked the Father what he would call his work. He answered me promptly: 'Relief of Suffering.' "

By 1946, about $6,000.00 had been collected. But war-time inflation devalued it to 1/80th of its pre-war value. Padre Pio and his nucleus of believers never lost hope.

Then in 1946, Miss Barbara Ward, a noted author from London, visited San Giovanni Rotondo. She was so impressed by Padre Pio and his plans that she later spoke to Fiorello LaGuardia, the ex-mayor of New York City and Director General of UNRRA. Her initiative resulted in a grant of about $340,000.00 from UNRRA funds.

Most of the money for the hospital was donated by people from the United States. The *Americani* were very dear to the heart of Padre Pio because of this self-sacrificing generosity. Along the length of its roof the hospital flies the flags of the nations which helped in its construction. The American flag flies proudly in the center, second only to the Italian flag.

Toward the end of 1947, the last beams of the hospital were in place. The out-patient department was opened in 1954 and full hospital facilities in 1956.

Other than Padre Pio, the masterminds of the Casa were Dr. William Sanguinetti, and a self-taught engineer, Angelo Lupi, a man with only an elementary school education. Padre Pio had reasons of his own for choosing Lupi over many professional engineers. His choice proved wise. Lupi quarried lime and stone from the mountains for do-it-yourself construction for bath tubs, sinks, bowls, indoor and outdoor tiles and paneling. He built a special lime kiln, and from the stone he extracted lime for the plaster. From scaffolding and from left-over wood he fabricated the finest furniture. He made the iron beds and wrought iron furnishings.

Because there was no water on the site, Lupi constructed a tie-in with the aqueduct of Apulia. Also, he built large cisterns and collected rain water from the terrace. For electricity, he erected a power plant with a diesel-driven generator. His ingenuity saved a fortune and produced a magnificent and eminently functional building.

When the hospital was dedicated on May 5, 1956, it hosted an international seminar of the European Society of Cardiology. The president of the Society, Dr. Gustav Nylin, from Sweden, called the hospital "a magnificent work of charity."

"On this memorable day of the inauguration of this home," Dr. Nylin said, "we pay our deferential respects to Padre Pio, author of this magnificent work of charity. In his firm Faith and his love for neighbor, Padre Pio offers us a splendid example of self-denial in the service of humanity. This hospital is a tangible example of the Good Samaritan. With all our hearts we express the wish that God may bless Padre Pio's noble and merciful activity. It is in the capacity of President of the European Society of Cardiology that I have had the privilege of addressing you these few words."

Dr. Paul Dudley White, President Eisenhower's personal physician, officially represented the United States. "This hospital," he said, "more than any other in the world, seems to me to be suitable for the study of the relationship between the soul and sickness. Here, more than anywhere, progress can be made in the study of the psychosomatic."

Professor Wagersteen, another doctor from the United States, said: "Everything here is beautiful, good and wonderful, but it saddens me to think that in the world there is only one Padre Pio. It is a great pity that there are not more.''

Padre Pio laughed aloud and said: ''God forbid!'' and he covered his face.

If we consider the typical reserve of most doctors and of British doctors in particular, we may be surprised by the exuberance of Dr. Evans, from England: ''This is the finest weekend I have ever spent in my life, and my meeting with Padre Pio is the most important moment of my most important weekend. Thank you, Padre Pio.''

Padre Pio addressed the doctors on this occasion. ''What can I say?'' he began. ''You have come into the world in the same way as I, with a mission to fulfill. I speak to you of duty, at a time when everyone talks only of rights! I, as a religious and a priest, have a mission to accomplish. As a religious and a Capuchin, I am bound to the perfect and strict observance of my Rule and vows. As a priest, mine is a mission of atonement, of propitiating God for the sins of mankind.

''All this may come to pass if I am in God's grace. But if I go astray from God, how can I make amends for others? How can I become a mediator with the Most High?

''You have the mission of curing the sick. But if at the patient's bedside you do not bring the warmth of loving care, I do not think that medicines will be of much use. I can prove this from my own experience. During my illness in 1916-1917, my doctors, while curing me, brought me words of consolation.

''Love cannot do without words. And you yourselves, how can you, other than by words, bring spiritual comfort to a patient?

''Later on I went to a specialist, who told me bluntly that I had tuberculosis and that I had only about another year to live. I returned home, grieved to death, but resigned to God's will. As you can see, I am still here! The specialist's prophecy did not come true. But not all patients are like Padre Pio of 1916-1917.

"Bring God to the sick! It will be more valuable than any other cure. And may the Lord bless you all, your families, and particularly your work and your patients. This is the most ardent wish of a priest's heart."

One of the Brothers who was among the closest to Padre Pio remarked to me: "I've often thought that Our Lord gave him such an extraordinary charitable work as the hospital to give him an interest in *something* on this earth."

Since its opening, the Casa has graduated over 300 registered nurses from its School of Nursing. A maintenance staff of 165 cleans the entire tile and marble hospital twice a day. The total hospital staff is 507. A lady from New York City, who went there just for treatment, said that "the cleanliness of the hospital amounted almost to an obsession with the maintenance personnel."

The rates per day for a hospital bed are about $14.75. Most patients are covered by insurance. But if they are not, their bills are covered by the *Stelline*, the Little Stars of Charity, to which people from all over the world contribute.

Two Capuchin priests serve as full-time chaplains. However, the total administration of the Casa Sollievo is now directly in the hands of the Vatican. Until his death in 1968, Padre Pio was its administrator. Then the Holy See appointed Monsignor Oreste Vighetti as administrator, and he continues in that office today.

When Padre Pio died, many people feared the hospital's financial collapse. With Padre Pio gone, who would contribute to his work? But when I visited San Giovanni Rotondo in 1971, I saw three wings under construction, for obstetrics, gynecology, and pediatrics. Plans were being made for additional departments for the treatment of eyes and mental health.

One year after the dedication of the hospital, Padre

Pio revealed a broader view which he had for the Casa. It was to be a motherhouse, the first among other institutions, like a lioness bearing and nourishing her cubs.

First of all, he envisioned the development of the hospital itself. "The Home must increase the number of its beds. There must be added two houses, one for women and one for men, where tired souls and bodies will come to the Lord and receive relief from Him.

"We must develop this work, so that it shall become a powerhouse of prayer and science, where the human race shall find peace in Jesus Crucified in one fold under one shepherd."

He urged that "priests and doctors feel the burning desire to continue the love of God in the work of charity among the sick, so that both they and their patients may live together in Him Who is Light and Love."

He envisioned a whole "hospital city technically adequate to meet the most advanced medical and surgical demands."

He envisioned "an international center of studies, which will enable doctors to further their professional studies and their formation as Christians."

He envisioned a retreat house where "priests will find here their Upper Room." He envisioned a home for "religious men and women, who will attend even more to their spiritual formation and assent to God so that in Faith, in detachment, and in self-surrender they may live the love of God, the consummation of Christian perfection."

He envisioned a hospital-home for the spastic and retarded children, a home for retired priests, homes for the aged, nurseries and day-care centers for children, and a Way of the Cross off the Viale Cappuccini.

He envisioned what we might call the Religious and Medical Center of Europe.

All of these projects were dear to Padre Pio's heart. Understandably so, because he said: "They are not only my works, but God's just as He shows me."

Some of these projects are already in operation. The retreat house is now open and can accommodate thirty retreatants. Down the Viale Cappuccini is the Center for Spastic and Retarded Children. In 1971 and 1972, two more Centers for Spastic Rehabilitation were opened in Manfredonia and Termoli respectively.

The Spastic Center in San Giovanni Rotondo also serves as one of the four day-care centers for small boys and girls. Another of these nurseries provides a boarding school for boys and girls. Staffed by four different Orders of nuns, all four centers are under the umbrella of the Capuchin friars.

Padre Pio lived to see work begin on the new Way of the Cross. Now completed, the Stations were executed in bronze by the internationally famous Francesco Messina. Although he was on in years, he eagerly accepted Padre Pio's invitation, because he wanted to dedicate his last great creation to Padre Pio. The path for the Way of the Cross meanders along the side of the mountain behind the church and hospital, crisscrossing a single flight of steps which stab straight up the flank of the mountain. Unfortunately, Padre Pio died before this Monumental Way of the Cross was dedicated by Cardinal Ursi in 1971.

There is another cub of the lioness which we have not yet mentioned, namely the Prayer Groups. He envisioned them, too, in 1957, as centers "in every part of the world where the children of the Casa Sollievo can join together to pray according to the spirit of the Seraphic Father St. Francis and according to the directives and the intentions of the Pope."

The hub of these Prayer Groups is the Casa itself, because he saw the Casa as the lioness and the Prayer Groups as cubs at her breast. That is why he referred to the members of the Prayer Groups as "Children of the Work." He said that his spiritual children "must find here the common home of their Prayer Groups." On July

31, 1968, shortly before Padre Pio's death, the Prayer Groups were given official recognition by the Vatican. Their director, appointed by the Congregation for Religious, was Padre Carmelo, the Capuchin Superior of Our Lady of Grace Friary.

Today, the Prayer Groups number about 900, with about 70,000 members. Because of their affiliation with the Casa, the Prayer Groups, like the Casa, are no longer under the direction of the Capuchins but immediately under Monsignor Oreste Vighetti, the Director of the Casa. He is an appointee of the Vatican.

Padre Pio said that if his spiritual children would meet to promote a prayer life, they would advance in the spiritual life. Today, the Prayer Groups continue as he established them, with an affiliation with the Casa.

There is no set agenda for the meetings of the Prayer Groups. Their program is worked out by the spiritual director. The only rules Padre Pio gave the Prayer Groups were: common prayer, charity, obedience to the Church and perseverance. It would be hard to list any virtues which were more typical of the spirituality of the Wise Man himself.

The Prayer Groups generally meet for one hour each month, in a home, a chapel or church or parish hall. Their membership includes priests, religious and laity. They observe what Padre Pio specified: they pray for the Church, for the Pope, for world peace, and especially for the patients in the Home for the Relief of Suffering. Now, after his death, they pray for Padre Pio's speedy glorification.

In the United States, many groups include the Sacrifice of the Mass at their meetings. Some groups conduct a Holy Hour, with exposition and Benediction of the Blessed Sacrament. Others recite fifteen decades of the rosary, with or without a short meditation before each decade. Still others recite common prayers from a booklet, especially the prayers which were recited by Padre

Pio in the Church of Our Lady of Grace. The spiritual director always gives a short sermon.

Some groups have a social after the meeting, perhaps with slides or films on Padre Pio and his works.

In theory, no officers are necessary. But it is usually wise to have a leader and perhaps a secretary, over and above the spiritual director, to help in the planning and administration of the meetings. If freewill offerings are collected, a treasurer will be necessary, perhaps to offer the spiritual director a stipend for his Mass and a donation to the pastor for the use of the parish facilities.

The Capuchins in San Giovanni Rotondo are anxious, almost to the point of mania, that the name of Padre Pio never be used for fund raising. Few people, however, see any danger in the sale of rosaries or literature, pictures and other small items about Padre Pio.

The Prayer Groups have no initiation ceremony, no period of probation, no dues. Only a willingness to pray and to co-operate with the group leader and the spiritual director.

Each group must be registered at the Casa Sollievo in San Giovanni Rotondo. (The address will be found in the epilog of this book.) No Prayer Group may be established without the express permission of the pastor of the parish in which they will meet. No Prayer Group may be started without a priest as the spiritual director.

"Padre Pio prayed that Prayer Groups would become beacons of light throughout the world," says Padre Lino Barbati, the Capuchin Superior of the Convento at San Giovanni Rotondo. "We have Prayer Groups all over the world, in the United States, Germany, England, Ireland, France, Switzerland, all over the world.

"People who did not know Father while he was alive, have come to recognize him after his death. Through the Prayer Groups, through his spiritual children, one person will speak of him and another will carry the message."

In this section on Padre Pio's Prayer Groups, a

group which calls itself "The Friends of Padre Pio" is worthy of special note. Among the nine hundred Prayer Groups around the world, this group is perhaps unique. Not only did it begin in 1957 at the direct intervention of Padre Pio, but also it is promoting a project which was approved and blessed by Padre Pio himself, namely, a Mental Health Institute in Italy. Its aim is the integration of psychotherapy and medicine with spiritual and moral assistance. Under Dr. Emilio Dido, its President, and Father Armand Dasseville, its Capuchin spiritual director, the Friends of Padre Pio remain distinct and separate from the works of the Casa and the Capuchins in San Giovanni Rotondo. "If they have the necessary financial means," Padre Pio told Angelo Battisti, who at the time was the Vatican-appointed Director of the Casa Sollievo, "we can give them any other assistance."

CHAPTER 15

Twilight, Death and Burial

Padre Pio forecast his death nine years before he died. He told Pietruccio, his blind friend, that he would die in his eighty-second year. When Padre Pio died on September 23, 1968, he was three months into his eighty-second year.

In 1959, when the new church at San Giovanni Rotondo was dedicated, a lady from Naples approached Padre Pio, very distressed. She felt certain that the blessing of the new church was an omen of his death. "No," he reassured her, "I'll die when they bless the crypt."

The crypt to which he referred was a room which had been excavated beneath the sanctuary of the church to serve as Padre Pio's tomb.

One day Padre Romolo sprang a question on Padre Pio: "Are you afraid of death?"

Padre Pio reflected for a moment. Then he said, almost flippantly: "No." He had been praying for his death all his life.

Several times, during the last three years of his life, he seemed to be at death's door. His health had deteriorated, and the bleeding of all his wounds had begun to lessen. He no longer came to the dining room for any meals. He moved about less.

Priests and Brothers were assigned to care for him around the clock. They always kept the intercom turned on, and, as his health ebbed, they remained with him in his room.

"In the last three years of his life," a Brother told me, "his thoughts started to close in on him. He would do nothing but pray."

About one year before he died, Padre Carmelo remarked: "Padre, you don't smile any more."

Dr. Sala, his personal physician, wrote: "In 1967 he had his first attacks of asthma, which greatly reduced his respiratory capacity. He often commented that his chest felt as though it were being crushed."

On July 7, 1968, his physical health collapsed. He recovered, but his strength was never the same. Often he was unable to offer Mass. He preferred to be alone. When he couldn't work, he spent his whole day in his room, in prayer. His five wounds stopped bleeding almost completely. His system was running out of blood. He could get around only in a wheelchair.

He was assigned a different and larger room down the corridor, 6 by 18 feet, with two windows overlooking the cloister garden. The room today is no longer protected by the monastery enclosure. It is kept just as it was when he died, except for the plastic with which the Capuchins had to cover everything.

A threadbare carpet partially covers the wooden floor. On the right as you enter is the small armchair in which he died. Next to it stands a little writing table, with a rosary, a relic of the True Cross, a few medals, and some candy which he used to give to the children who came to see him. A magnesia snuffbox, old and worn, also stands on the table, one which he never got around to giving away.

Opposite the door is his bed. At its head hangs a

wooden crucifix, and nearby are the intercom and a little picture of Christ being taken down from the Cross. His sandals, which he wore to the hour of his death, still remain on the floor near his bed as though waiting for him to slip into them again.

On the north wall to the left are pictures of the Sacred Heart, St. Michael the Archangel, Our Lady of Lourdes, and Our Lady of Libera, who is venerated in Pietrelcina. There are also pictures of Dr. William Sanguinetti, Angelo Lupi and Maria Pyle, and two olive branches with a picture of his parents in the center.

There is a lamp on an end table, partially covered with a brown cloth. Padre Pio had arranged it very precisely, so that it could throw a ray of light onto the picture of Pope Paul VI. The table also has a rosary on it, and a book of meditations on the Passion of Jesus, by Father Gaetano of Bergamo. Padre Pio read that book frequently. There are also a comb, a letter opener, a fountain pen, a hearing aid which he sometimes used during his last days, and a Westclox alarm clock stopped at 3:42.

Near the foot of his bed hangs a picture of Our Lady, with the Infant in her lap.

As I left the room, I was startled to see a cupboard with the medical kit which held his injections. I noticed also the cup from which he was offered a sip of coffee just before he died. With these mementos stands a little statue of St. Francis embracing the crucifix.

Call it coincidence, call it Divine Providence, but the weekend of his death thousands of visitors were in San Giovanni Rotondo to celebrate the fiftieth anniversary of his stigmata, the blessing of the Monumental Way of the Cross, the blessing of the crypt, and the official recognition of his Prayer Groups by the Vatican. Father Armand Dasseville and Father Didacus Joseph Moran, two Capuchins from the New York Province, were there with sixty spiritual children from their Province.

Friday
September 20

Friday, September 20, was the fiftieth anniversary of Padre Pio's stigmata. Fifty precious vases with deep red roses given by his spiritual children almost blanketed the altar, the sanctuary and the side balconies of the church.

Padre Pio offered Mass as usual at 5:00 a.m. The church was full. Father Armand told me: "I could see his wounds."

In the afternoon he participated in the recitation of the rosary and Benediction of the Blessed Sacrament. But he got through his day more through will power than with bodily strength.

"I wish you another fifty years," Father Romolo said to him.

Padre Pio, perhaps seriously, answered him: "What harm have I ever done to you?"

In the evening, he had another asthma attack, but it passed without any apparent serious complications.

Saturday
September 21

The next day, Saturday, September 21, he was too ill to offer Mass. But again he snapped back.

Dr. Sala describes what kind of a day he had. "At five o'clock in the morning of September 21, he had a very bad attack of bronchial asthma, together with tachycardia (a racing heart), cold sweating, labial cyanosis (his lips turned blue), and a decrease in arterial pressure. Therapeutic treatment immediately undertaken was successful. Later in the morning, Padre Pio was able to sit on the veranda and pray. He was lively and smiling, with Padre Onorato and his doctor."

Later in the afternoon, Padre Pio attended the rosary service and Benediction of the Blessed Sacrament in the church, but he spent most of his day in his room, in prayer.

Sunday   On Sunday, September 22, Padre Pio
September 22   did not think he had the strength to
offer Mass. Padre Carmelo registered
disappointment. The large church was
already jammed with pilgrims from all over the world.
Padre Pio interpreted Padre Carmelo's reaction as a
command of obedience, and he began Mass.

At that Mass, for the first time he seemed unconcerned about letting the wounds of his hands be seen.
Even though he had never been able completely to conceal them at Mass in previous years, he had always tried
to cover them with the long sleeves of his habit and alb.
But now there was almost nothing to see. The bleeding
had stopped, the wounds were almost invisible.

"As he went out to say Mass on the morning of September 22," a Brother told me, "I found some white or
light pink crusts of blood or dried skin in the sacristy.
There was a tone of pink in them, very pale pink, not
crusted with blood, but more or less dried skin. They
could have been the last layers of skin which had dried
out, with the skin beneath coming back to normal. Or
they could have been pieces of blood, or serum, which
chipped off from the stigmata. Maybe the wounds closed
that morning. I don't know when they closed. I don't
think anyone knows exactly. No one could know, unless
Padre Pio revealed it to his confessor, but his confessor
could never reveal it."

Padre Pio walked to the altar and not only said Mass,
he *sang it*, along with two assistants. He coughed and
gasped for breath, but that was common enough. There
was no special reason for alarm. His voice was a bit
shaky, but in general it was as vigorous as ever. At Mass
he gave First Holy Communion to a boy and two girls.

Suddenly, after the blessing at the end of Mass, he
collapsed. The crowd gasped and surged forward as far
as the Communion rail. His brethren, always at his side,

caught him. Within a few moments, while still standing at the altar, he recovered.

He turned around to leave the altar and accepted the offer of a wheelchair which someone had hastily brought into the sanctuary. As he was wheeled away, he looked back to the people in the church and stretched out his arms as though he wanted to embrace them. He was heard to murmur: "My children, my children."

He made his thanksgiving as usual in the sacristy, and then started into the church to hear the confessions of the women. But he had to turn back. He returned to his room. On the way he stopped at the choir window and blessed the crowd in the piazza beneath him.

Later that morning, to everyone's surprise, he insisted on going downstairs to hear confessions of the men. The appointment roster had not been called out in the church, and most people had left. He heard the confessions of only a few men.

He spoke for awhile to the few women who had come into the old sacristy to meet him. One of them, Miss Cleonice Morcaldi, described for me what it was like. "We kissed his hand, but he could hardly sit erect in his chair. He had a cadaverous look. I said: 'Padre, please say something to us.'

"He stretched his arms out and said: 'I love everyone equally. Unfortunately, I am not received kindly by everyone.' "

Representatives from 726 Prayer Groups had gathered in San Giovanni Rotondo. At 8:00 a.m., sixteen priests offered a concelebrated Mass presided over by Bishop Antonio Cunial. Padre Pio was unable to attend the Mass.

At 10:00 a.m., Padre Clemente of S. Maria in Punto, a Definitor General from Rome, blessed the crypt. Nobody suspected that before the week was over Padre Pio's body would occupy that tomb.

The Prayer Groups had scheduled a meeting for

10:30 a.m. A little after ten o'clock, Padre Pio again came to the choir window and blessed his people. He had to be held up by two friars.

"He looked terrible," Father Armand said. "His face was clearly marked by great suffering, unsmiling. He waved his handkerchief lightly, but the usual enthusiasm of recognizing the people was lacking. It was worse in the afternoon. His eyes were glassy, and he stared ahead as if into the next world. His features seemed already set in the immobility of death. . . . Everyone was thinking and asking the same question: 'Is this the end?' "

At the meeting of the Prayer Groups, Padre Carmelo read a telegram from the Vatican which announced their official recognition and approval.

Padre Pio did not eat lunch. He merely tasted it. Then he went to bed. At 1:00 o'clock in the afternoon he said the Our Father aloud.

At 3:30 o'clock, Padre Clemente blessed the first stone of the Monumental Way of the Cross. A meditation was read at each Station by laymen from several countries.

Later in the afternoon, a new project dear to the heart of Padre Pio was revealed by the famous Enrico Medi, professor of terrestrial physics of the University of Rome, former Vice President of Euratom (the European Atomic Committee) and member of the Pope's special consulting committee. He also represented the Pope at the activities that weekend. He brought from the Vatican the official approval of a plan for construction of a school in San Giovanni Rotondo to form the laity according to the guidelines of the Second Vatican Council.

During the afternoon, Padre Pio refused to stay in bed. He sat up in his chair in the sun parlor near his room. When the bell sounded for Benediction of the Blessed Sacrament at 4:30 p.m., he responded immediately. It was to be his last. He was weak and in pain, but he remained until the end.

After Benediction, Padre Pio again blessed the people who crowded beneath his window. He then retired to bed.

That Sunday evening, at 9:00 o'clock, Padre Pio summoned Padre Pellegrino on the intercom. Padre Pellegrino found him in tears. All Padre Pio wanted to know was the time. Five or six times after that, between 9:00 o'clock and midnight, he kept calling Padre Pellegrino. His eyes were red from weeping. He kept on asking what time it was. Still, there was no special reason to be alarmed at his condition.

Monday September 23 12:00 A.M. At midnight, Padre Pio again summoned Padre Pellegrino and begged him to stay with him. "He was like a frightened child," Padre Pellegrino said. "His eyes were begging me, his hands clenched mine."

As if he had forgotten how often he had asked the time, he again asked Padre Pellegrino: "My son, did you offer Mass yet?" Padre Pellegrino patiently repeated that it was too early.

"Well," Padre Pio responded, "this morning you will offer it for me."

Then he insisted on going to confession. At the end, he said: "My son, if the Lord calls me today, ask my brethren to forgive me for all the trouble I have caused them, and ask my brethren and my spiritual children to pray for my soul."

Padre Pellegrino reached for words with which to answer him. "Father," he said, "I am sure that the Lord will let you live for a long time yet, but if you are right, may I ask you for a last blessing for the brethren, for the spiritual children, and for your patients?"

"Yes," Padre Pio agreed, "I bless them all. Ask the

superior to give them this last blessing for me.''

Then he asked Padre Pellegrino to recite the words of his religious profession, his vows of poverty, chastity and obedience. He repeated them word for word: ''I, Padre Pio of Pietrelcina, vow and promise to Almighty God, to the Blessed Virgin Mary, to our holy Father St. Francis, to all the saints and to you, Father, to observe all the days of my life, the Rule of the Friars Minor, confirmed by Pope Honorius, and living in obedience, without property, and in chastity.''

Padre Pellegrino answered with the usual words: ''And I, on the part of God, if you observe these things, promise you everlasting life.''

Padre Pio was having trouble breathing, but that had been a lifelong problem. There was still no indication of any imminent danger.

At about 1:30 a.m., Padre Pio asked Padre Pellegrino to help him get out of bed. He exchanged his pajamas for his Franciscan habit and walked into the sun parlor next door. To Padre Pellegrino's amazement, he walked with the step of a young man. Padre Pellegrino had only to escort him. Padre Pio snapped on the light and sat down.

Five minutes later, he wanted to get up again and return to his room. This time he could not stand by himself. Padre Pellegrino had to lift him into his wheelchair and return him to his room.

Padre Pio sat down in the armchair. ''I see two Mothers,'' he said. Then a strange pallor spread over his face. Beads of sweat formed on his brow. His breathing became labored. His lips turned livid. He kept repeating: ''*Gesú, Maria,*'' but with an ever weakening voice.

Padre Pellegrino realized that his Spiritual Father was in serious trouble and made a move for the door.

Padre Pio stopped him. ''Don't call anyone,'' Padre Pio said. But Padre Pellegrino decided to go anyway.

He had taken only a few steps out of the room when

Padre Pio called him back. "I didn't think he was calling me to say the same thing over again, so I went back to him," Padre Pellegrino later reported.

"Don't call anyone," Padre Pio insisted.

"Father, let me go," Padre Pellegrino begged, and he ran to Brother Bill Martin's room. "Padre Pio is ill," he told the Brother.

Immediately Brother Bill (now Father Giuseppe Pio) went to Padre Pio's room, and Padre Pellegrino summoned Doctor Sala. Within ten minutes the doctor arrived. They put Padre Pio to bed. The doctor checked his vital signs and gave an injection for severe asthma. Then they lifted the Padre into the armchair. Padre Pio kept repeating: "Jesus, Mary," but his voice almost trailed away.

Padre Pio's heart was palpitating. Another injection, this one directly into his heart. The spark of life almost went out. Two more doctors arrived and stood beside him, together with the Capuchin priests and Brothers. Padre Paolo administered the Sacrament of Anointing of the Sick. The doctor gave him oxygen. The Capuchins recited the prayers for the dying.

Padre Pio was still conscious and calm. But his features had become waxen. His hands and feet and face were cold. His pulse weakened. He bent his head slightly to the left and closed his eyes. He no longer responded to the doctor's voice.

"Padre! Padre!" the doctor shouted.

He opened his eyes, looked wistfully at the doctor and again closed his eyes. He was still breathing. The death rattle began in his throat.

At 2:09 he stopped breathing. The doctor administered external heart massage and with the help of a respirator Padre Pio again began to breathe. But his eyes showed no reflexes.

"At half past two," according to Doctor Gusso, "the

clinical signs of death, the most peaceful and sweet I have ever seen, were present.''

In Doctor Sala's words: ''At half past two, with an imperceptible turn of the head to the right and a weak sigh, Padre Pio, his face distended, pale, bloodless, his lips slightly parted, like a little bird, died.''

Everyone except Doctor Sala, Padre Carmelo, Padre Pellegrino and three friars left the room. While they washed and clothed the body of Padre Pio in his Capuchin habit, an almost white scab about two inches long detached itself from his left hand.

They saw that the stigmata had completely disappeared! Not even a scar remained. Only a red mark as if drawn by a red pencil remained on his side. Then that, too, disappeared.

Even in death, Padre Pio acknowledged the loving service of Doctor Sala.

''As I was clothing Padre Pio's body,'' the doctor said, ''with the same habit that he wore before dying, I smelled the same strong scent of orange blossoms which I had often perceived during my almost daily encounters with Padre Pio.''

Within one hour of Padre Pio's death, Padre Giacomo photographed his hands and feet and side. The sharp pictures corroborated the words of Padre Lino: ''After his death, the wounds receded from his body. As the warmth left his body, less was seen of his wounds. As the body got colder, the wounds seemingly closed up. They receded. His hands and his feet became smooth. The skin was as smooth as a baby's skin, with no trace of blood.''

As with the Apostles, who realized what Jesus had said about His death and Resurrection only after the events happened, a Brother recalled that many years previously a woman had prayed to Padre Pio: ''Padre Pio, Padre Pio, please cure me. Cure me. I am sick. I have gone to many hospitals, but no one seems to help me.''

Everyone tried to quiet her. Padre Pio drew near and asked her: "What do you want?"

"I am sick," she repeated. "I have gone to many doctors, but no one has been able to cure me. I am a mother with children. Cure me! Cure me!"

"My child," Padre Pio answered her, "I, too, was born sick. I lived sick."

Then he turned to the Brother and said: "But I will die healthy (*sano*: healthy or whole). Even my hands will be clean of the wounds."

Newspapers around the world immediately printed the news of his death. Some of them reported that the wounds had disappeared before his death. But Padre Pellegrino took sharp exception to those statements.

"Many newspapers," he charged, "had published the news that Padre Pio's wounds had disappeared toward the end of his life. Without any presumption I can honestly state that no one knows the truth in this regard better than myself, since I was at Padre Pio's side until the very last moment.

"Hence, I can testify that the stigmata had not disappeared as reported. Factually, they were visible until his death. However, I can clarify this mistaken report by stating that for the last four months of Padre Pio's life, the wounds no longer bled at all, and only on rare occasions did they shed just a few drops of blood. This is accounted for by his extreme anemia."

The disappearance of the stigmata caused no consternation among the priests or the laity.

"They were signs to help the ministry of Padre Pio," said his lifelong friend, Padre Onorato. "The ministry was finished, so the signs were finished."

Miss Morcaldi reflected the sentiments of many of his spiritual children: "On the day of his death, his wounds were completely healed. His hands were like those of a child. This, of course, impressed us very much. God wounded him and God cured him."

A strange thing happened the night of Padre Pio's death. Two elderly but very alert ladies from Rome were sharing a room in a hotel in San Giovanni Rotondo. One of them had been especially upset. "Don't you hear how the dogs are howling?" she remarked.

"I sat on my bed and heard it too," her companion Miss Hamilton told me. "In Tuscany we call that the howling of death. We heard it perfectly. Then at midnight we went to sleep."

"At half past two," Miss Hamilton continued, "Giovanna suddenly woke up screaming: 'The Father is dying, the Father is dying!'

"Giovanna," Miss Hamilton told her, "you had a bad dream. Please keep quiet."

Miss Hamilton looked at her watch. "Be quiet," she told Giovanna. "It is half past two."

"No, no, no, no, no, no," Giovanna said. "I have seen Padre Pio!"

"Where was he?" Miss Hamilton asked.

"I don't know," Giovanna answered. "They were all looking down, lined up in a straight row. I saw seven Capuchins. Two men were dressed in white. Evidently they were doctors. I must go and see."

"Giovanna," Miss Hamilton protested, "please! Are you going to go out in the middle of the night?"

Giovanna put on a wrap and fled out of the room. Then Miss Hamilton heard her scream. She sprang out of bed, rushed outside into the garden and saw Giovanna running toward her, screaming: "The Padre is dead! The Padre is dead! We are orphans! We are orphans! We will never see him again."

Miss Hamilton expected her companion to have a heart attack. She rushed to her and took her in her arms. "Giovanna," she said, "keep still. You mustn't yell like that. You will disturb the whole place."

She led her back to their hotel room. "I don't know if the Padre is dead," Miss Hamilton scolded her, "but if he is dead, I'm sure he wouldn't want you to act this way. You are not showing that you believe the way we should believe. You mustn't behave like this. Even if he is dead, from this moment Padre Pio will be judged on how we behave. You can't carry on like this. You must be like the women of the Gospel, and not like a neurotic."

"Yes," Giovanna answered her, "I know it. But please for charity's sake, go and see if it is true. Many times in the past Padre Pio was very seriously ill, and suddenly he got well again. Go and see if it is true."

Miss Hamilton dressed hurriedly and rushed to the piazza outside the convento.

"The first thing I saw," she told me, "was the police. The *carabiniere* were already there. They had never been there that early in the morning. It wasn't even 3:00 o'clock.

She spoke to one of them. "Please," she pleaded, "is it true that the Padre is dead?"

"I know nothing," the policeman answered her. "I know nothing. I know nothing until the sun rises. That is the order I have received."

Miss Hamilton approached the police captain but he said the same thing: "I know nothing. I may not speak."

"Please tell me, please tell me for charity's sake," Miss Hamilton insisted.

He said: "Look at me!"

"He was weeping," Miss Hamilton told me slowly and deliberately. "All his uniform . . ." She could not easily continue, but she was not crying. She showed marvelous control for a lady eighty-one years of age.

At noon, the proprietor of the hotel returned to their room. "I have come to thank you," he said to Miss Hamilton.

He was referring to the events of 2:30 that morning. When he had heard Giovanna screaming and Miss Hamilton trying to quiet her, he went to their room and asked if he could help. His daughter who accompanied him stood behind him.

Miss Hamilton simply said: "No. *Il Padre e morto.* The Padre is dead."

The proprietor turned white. Miss Hamilton closed the door on them.

"I have come to thank you," he told Miss Hamilton when he returned at noon. "It was a great shock to me when you told me last night that Padre Pio was dead. But my daughter was there, and she immediately gave me what I needed for my heart. After a while I was well again. If I had gone out and learned it any other way, I'd have fallen down dead."

Recapitulating the whole incident, Miss Hamilton said: "Even in what happened, I cannot say that there was anything extraordinary. Things happened in a way they never happened before, but nobody was hurt. Nobody. It was the most terrible night. It was terrible, I'll never forget it if I live a hundred and fifty years."

Later Monday afternoon, the body of Padre Pio was waked in an open wooden casket, near the Communion rail in the church, in full view. On Tuesday that casket was replaced by a metal casket having a clear glass cover.

"He looked so peaceful," Father Armand remarked. "He didn't seem dead, but rather asleep as he lay there with his arms across his chest."

A rosary was entwined around his hands. His hands were covered with the brown fingerless mittens the people were used to seeing him wear.

Pope Paul VI sent a telegram to the Capuchins: "The august Pontiff has heard with fatherly sorrow of the passing away of Padre Pio of Pietrelcina, and he prays the Lord to grant His faithful servant an eternal crown of justice. The Holy Father sends his apostolic blessing and condolences to the religious community in their sorrow, to the doctors, the staff, the patients of the Home for the

Relief of Suffering, and to the whole population of San Giovanni Rotondo.''

The body of Padre Pio was waked in the church until Thursday, September 26, when he was buried. Before the burial Mass, there was a funeral procession through the town.

About 100,000 people lined the mile-and-a-half route. The villagers had draped their best tablecloths and Persian rugs and bedspreads from the windows and rooftops, and many displayed huge pictures of their beloved Padre. All the people in town wore their Sunday best.

"I saw many men and women, priests and religious," Father Armand recalled, "unashamedly and in public view wipe tears away. They tossed flowers from the windows, and flowers were dropped from the helicopter which hovered over the cortege. 'Padre Pio, Padre Pio,' some cried, and there were a few outbursts of grief. Yet, strangely, everyone commented, the procession was well ordered and there was no hysteria."

At the *Municipio,* the city Hall, the mayor, Dr. Sala, gave a eulogy. Father Didacus Joseph Moran told me: "When the Mayor was reading the eulogy, I thought that at first he couldn't see his paper, but he was crying. He broke down while he was giving his talk."

In front of the hearse was Father Clementinus, the General Superior of the Capuchin Order. Padre Pio's companions from the friary formed an honor guard around the casket. Representatives of other religious Orders, the secular clergy, and local and national government officials joined the procession. Hundreds of Capuchins, including novices, participated. This marked the first time novices had been permitted to participate in such an event.

The doctors from the Casa Sollievo participated as a group. "They showed the profoundest grief," Father Didacus Joseph said. "It was nothing put on."

Father Didacus told me of a Capuchin whom he met,

who had been stationed in San Giovanni Rotondo. "He was crying to break his heart. He said: 'I loved him. He was so good to me.' "

Father Clementinus concelebrated the outdoor funeral Mass with twenty-six Capuchin friars and two Bishops. The police locked hands to contain the crowd that surged forward. After the Mass, the hearse bore the casket to the Casa Sollievo for a final salute to the hospital's founder.

At 10:30 p.m., the casket, now with its metal cover in place, was carried down the double marble stairway of the crypt. It was buried in the center of the floor and covered with a seven-ton rectangular block of black and white speckled marble. At 10:00 a.m. the following day, Friday, September 27, the crypt was opened to the public.

The crypt is a 69 x 90-foot room located beneath the sanctuary of the church. Lantern-like electric lights jut from the beige painted, rough concrete walls or hang down from the seven massive arches. The 30-foot ceiling doesn't appear to be as high as it actually is. It is hard to tell that the beams across the ceiling are only plaster resembling golden oak.

As soon as the crypt was open to the public, an unending stream of visitors began. They were returning to visit their Padre, their host and their friend who, though dead, is very much alive.

CHAPTER 16

Life Through Death

In 1967, the United Press International estimated that one and a half million people visited Padre Pio that year. On Easter Sunday, 1968, Padre Pio himself gave Holy Communion to over 700 people.

"Watch when I die," Padre Pio predicted. "You will see even more *chiasso!*"

Now after Padre Pio's death, the crypt, the convento, the Casa, and the whole town are still vibrant.

The present volume of mail to the convento averages seventy letters a day from English-speaking countries alone, from the United States, England, Ireland, Australia, Ceylon, and Pakistan.

Prophets of gloom who predicted that San Giovanni Rotondo would become a ghost town were so wrong. During 1970, there were three million visitors to San Giovanni Rotondo, double the UPI estimate of 1967. When I was there in 1971, the Albergo (Hotel) Vittoria had just opened. The Albergo Gaggiano was less than two years old.

Along the Viale Cappuccini alone I counted seven hotels, six *pensioni* (boarding houses), and clusters of new five- and seven-story apartment buildings. In addition, many hotels and *pensioni* are located elsewhere in town. One hotel closed for a while after the death of Padre Pio, but its closing was due to personal family reasons, not to a decrease of pilgrims. It is now open again.

The construction of apartment houses and new homes makes San Giovanni Rotondo look like a boom town. Two new hotels are now under construction, and yet another is being enlarged. Residents and businessmen have confidence in a bright today and tomorrow.

I did not even try to count the religious goods shops. Most of them sell picture postcards, statuettes, slides of Padre Pio, and the usual cheap plastic calendar-art pictures of Jesus whose eyes open and close when you move to the left or to the right.

Fortunately, all the stores are at a respectful distance from the convento. There is only one exception, a little shop managed by the friars. But this lies off in the corner of the piazza, and you probably would never realize that it is a gift shop unless you should happen to stray into it by chance. I lived at the convento for a full week before I learned that it was a gift shop. I thought it was a workshop associated with the friary.

The church and crypt are also alive. Though there is still the quiet reverence befitting a holy place, there is a continuous flow of pilgrims. If you are attentive when you visit the crypt, you might spot the guest book off to the side. I counted the signatures of the people who had found it and had gone to the trouble of signing it. I counted 5,800 names signed during the first thirteen days of July, 1971.

The fourth of July is no special day in Italy. But on that day, I counted five buses and seventy-nine cars in the parking lot. It is unlikely that you will ever find the crypt empty until 8:00 p.m., when the church is locked. Even during the quieter hours, from noon till mid-afternoon, there is an average of about thirty people in the church or the crypt. If you were to tally up the number of people standing around "Padre Pio's tree" in the piazza or making the Way of the Cross, you would probably count close to a hundred people at any given time.

San Giovanni is a friendly town. Villagers do not rush out and glad-hand a visitor. But any pilgrim, I think, will be accepted by them as a person who belongs in their town. They assume that a visitor's feelings about Padre Pio run as deeply as their own.

On my visit I was impressed by the charity and spirituality which Padre Pio had formed among his people. I felt the warmth of their greeting: *"Pac' e bene,* Peace and everything good." That is the way they greeted me and each other.

Two little ragamuffins once ran up to me as I left the convento. Presuming that they were beggars, I instinctively reached into my pocket for some coins. But one of them wanted only to kiss the cross on my rosary. The other wanted only to kiss my hand, the hand of a priest. All the people kiss a priest's hand when they meet him. They will not let a priest deny them that. The two little urchins did their thing and scampered away on cloud nine.

When offering Mass in the church, I did not follow a schedule. I was completely on my own. But somehow, word always got around that a Mass was being offered, and within a few minutes a hundred or more people would appear in the church. They answered the prayers in Latin.

Should I be visiting with people when the Angelus rang at noon or at 6:00 o'clock, silence would fall immediately while they waited for me to recite the Angelus in Latin. They responded in Latin. I had not experienced anything like that since my seminary days.

I was also highly edified to see the church almost filled with people a half hour before Mass began. Many remained in thanksgiving for almost an hour after Mass. They responded with the same eagerness whenever the bell summoned them to the recitation of the rosary or Benediction of the Blessed Sacrament. Up the hill they came in force.

This devotion is part of them. It is not a show. Unless you look closely you may not see that they are praying their rosaries or praying the Stations of the Cross as they hike up the hill to the church.

I saw the same devotion at the crypt. No hours are assigned to any Capuchin to stand vigil. But I was deeply moved by their frequent visits. Morning, noon and night, young Capuchins who are in their studies at San Giovanni Rotondo, and older Capuchins who are still in active work or retired, drop in for a visit or to pray their rosary. Every evening I saw an elderly Capuchin priest who would leave his hospital bed and come over to visit his old friend.

Something else which may strike the visitor as strange is the total absence of any "funeral parlor" atmosphere. The dozen bouquets of fresh flowers which are always present don't make the crypt look or smell like a funeral home. Though the crypt is always quiet and stark with its unadorned walls and granite floor, with only a few chairs and kneelers, you can't help but feel that it is simply a visiting room where you can drop in and chat with your friend, Padre Pio.

At the crypt I saw a woman with her teen-age daughter. They sat on the kneeler of one of the benches, almost on the floor, facing each other in a crouch, as they whispered the rosary together.

There were a few elderly Italian ladies in their long black dresses and black shawls. But the strong accent, surprisingly, was on youth. Young men with long hair, young men with short hair, girls and young ladies, engaged couples and newlyweds, doctors and nurses, family groups, visiting priests and occasionally a Bishop or a

Cardinal, all formed the revolving scene of silent visitors.

Only as I left the crypt did I realize that there wasn't any picture of Padre Pio in the tomb. The only religious art consists of scenes from the life of Christ, sculptured into the marble bas-relief around the pillars and walls, and a life-size image of Jesus beneath the one altar in the crypt.

In all the weeks I was there, I didn't see a single display of hysteria, fanaticism, or unguarded emotion. The closest thing to hysteria I experienced was when a woman told me that she thought I looked like St. Anthony!

You will never see mini-skirts or men in shorts either in the church or in the crypt. They are rarely seen even in the town. Two men with blue arm-bands stand at the door of the church and politely but firmly inform visitors so attired that these styles are not acceptable there. They keep a supply of dark blue raincoats handy so that improperly dressed visitors will not have to be turned away.

Everybody who visits Padre Pio's "City on a Mountain" can feel the mantle of peace which enwraps the convento, the old church, the new church, the Casa, the piazza outside the convento, and the Way of the Cross. I tried to understand why this is so.

It was the little children especially who made me wonder. What kept them so happy and quiet? There is *nothing* there to entertain them. Yet, I didn't see a single child who was "fussy" or anxious to go home, even when the family remained there for the better part of a week. It became clear to me that the children, too, felt the soothing presence of Padre Pio. Children and adults — all were happy to be with their friend.

The whole scene made me think. Padre Pio was dead. But here were whole families, and this sinner, too, who *felt* his presence in the crypt.

Was this experience nothing more than our own subjective reaction? Was the warmth which we felt only the privilege of the comparatively few people who were enjoying the brilliance of a sun which has already set, whose light will fade into darkness when the sun dips deeper?

What about people who have never visited San Giovanni Rotondo? Will all the unusual stories about this strange Gladiator of the Gargano make people who feel no affection for him look on him, after all, as nothing more than a freak?

On the other hand, might there not be a message for the world in Padre Pio's life and death? Might not his life and death have a wider, broader meaning than a biographical one? Might not the glow in the hearts of visitors to his tomb be communicable to people elsewhere? Might not "Everyman" need him or at least find a lift in life through him?

I can think of no better way to answer those questions and to end this book on the Fourth Wise Man than to quote Padre Pio himself. I will share the major portion of a letter which he wrote in 1915 to his spiritual director:

> "Pietrelcina
> "July 1, 1915

"My Dearest Father,

"May Jesus fill your soul with the choicest graces and always let you feel more and more the sweetness of the cross which you bear as a Christian.

"How sweet, Father is the word cross! Here, at the foot of the cross, souls are clothed in light, they are set afire with love. Here they grow wings to fly aloft to the dizziest heights.

"May this cross always be for us the bed of our rest, the school of perfection, our dear inheritance. With this purpose in mind, let us take care not to separate the cross from the love of

Jesus. Otherwise one without the other would become an unbearable burden to our weakness.

"May Our Lady of Sorrows help us through her most holy Son always to penetrate deeper into the mystery of the cross and to become enraptured with her at the suffering of Jesus. The most certain proof of love consists in suffering for the one we love, and after the Son of God suffered so much torture out of sheer love, there can be no doubt that the cross which we carry for Him becomes as lovable as love.

"The most holy Virgin will obtain for us love of the cross, of suffering. And she who was the first to practice the Gospel in all its perfection, in all its severity, even before it was made public, will obtain for us and she herself will give to us the spur to move immediately to her side.

"Let us too, like so many elect souls, strive to remain always beside this Blessed Mother, to walk always by her side, there being no other road which leads to life other than that which was trod by Our Mother. Let us not reject this road, we who wish to reach the end.

"Let us always join with this dear Mother. Let us go with her beside Jesus outside of Jerusalem, the symbol of the field of the stubbornness of the Jews, of the world which rejects and denies Jesus Christ, and from which Jesus declared He was separated, when He said: 'I am not of the world,' and which He excluded from His prayer to the Father: 'I do not pray for the world.'. . .

"Yes, Father, let us leave Jerusalem the renegade, Jerusalem the God-killer, Jerusalem the unfaithful, and go out into the open field, walking next to Jesus as we carry the glorious infamy of His cross.

"We are invited to do this by the Apostles: 'Let us approach Him, therefore, outside of the camp carrying His burden.' We are also invited to do this by the Divine Master: 'Whoever wishes to come after me, let him deny himself, take up his cross, and follow me.' Let us always keep our gaze fixed on this noble, reverent and holy group which follows Jesus to Golgotha. There is not one person in that group who does not bear the profession of true Faith on his brow, self-denial in his heart, and the cross on his back. Let us find the courage to follow this adventurous group, in which all the consolations are united with all the sacrifices, with all the hopes and with all the virtues.

"We will meet when and where God wishes, and in the meanwhile, do not deny me your paternal, sincere blessing.

"Your poor son,
"Fra Pio, Capuchin"

CHAPTER 17

Epilog

1. *Canonization*

Canonization is the statement by which the Pope declares that a person is in heaven. The Pope canonizes a person only after an exhaustive study of his or her life. The study must prove that the person lived not only a good Christian life, but a *heroic* life, that is, that he or she stood up straight as Christians in spite of exceptional pressure. Only then can the person be called a saint.

A number of steps must be taken which lead up to the canonization of a saint. These steps are now being taken. In modern times, the Church does not follow a hard and fast timetable in this whole process. We know that at present everything is going extremely well in the cause for the canonization of Padre Pio. Please God, the final declaration will not be long hence.

2. *Addresses and Publications*

All persons who want to report a favor received through the prayer of Padre Pio are asked to contact the

Capuchins in San Giovanni, Italy. The address is:

> Postulator's Office for the Cause of Padre Pio
> Capuchin Monastery of Our Lady of Grace
> 71013 San Giovanni Rotondo
> (Foggia) Italy

A very attractive quarterly magazine entitled *The Voice of Padre Pio,* is published by the Postulator's Office, in several languages, replete with pictures and information on Padre Pio. There is no fixed subscription rate, but $4.00 a year would be a reasonable offering. Subscriptions to the English edition may be obtained by writing to:

> The Voice of Padre Pio
> c/o Mrs. Vera Calandra
> 11 N. Whitehall Rd.
> Norristown, Pa. 19401